Odd Days of Heaven

Odd Days

—— *of* ——

Heaven

More than 180 ways
to lift your spirits

SANDRA BRAY

LOCAL LEGEND SPIRITUAL WRITING
COMPETITION RUNNER-UP

A record of this publication is available from the British Library.

ISBN: 978-1-910027-17-2

Typesetting by Wordzworth Ltd
www.wordzworth.com

Cover design by Titanium Design Ltd
www.titaniumdesign.co.uk

Printed by Lightning Source UK
www.lightningsource.com

Cover image *The Birth of a Star*, an original painting by Alicia Box (acrylic on canvas)

Published by Local Legend
www.local-legend.co.uk

This book is dedicated to all animals,
for they enrich our lives.

Acknowledgements

My thanks to those whom I call my local spiritual heroes who, sometimes unknowingly, have helped me develop along my path at various stages, as without them this book would never have been written: Jan Phethean, Connie Osbourn, Julie Burke, Sally Parker, Alan Jones, Maureen Rolls, Ann Moore, Helen Stone, Mala Mandalia, Debbie Walker, Mary and Adrian Smith, Val Ives and Stephanie Parr. I must also mention my wonderful canine companion Twosocks as she too has enabled my spiritual journey in unusual ways.

I am greatly indebted to Nigel Peace of Local Legend for his expertise in guiding me in the completion of this book.

www.local-legend.co.uk

The Author

Sandra Bray grew up and lives in Cornwall, England, and is still inspired daily by the local seashore and countryside, as well as the region's Celtic traditions and folklore. She is often to be seen exercising her dog on the beach.

She has worked in industry and the Royal Air Force, as a college lecturer and for the National Health Service. But it was the loss of her father and brother within a few months that sparked an interest in complementary and alternative healing, leading her to become a Reiki Master and a practitioner of Natural and Vibrational Healing and Indian Head Massage, for both people and animals.

Sandra now volunteers Reiki healing each week at her local animal rescue centre and also reads the Tarot for local people at charity events, as well as facilitating workshops.

Sandra's website is *http://sange888.com*

This Book

Rocked by mid-life events and with her self-confidence bruised, Sandra refused to be a victim of her circumstances and instead decided to treat them as catalysts for positive change. This is exactly how we grow spiritually! This is how we find the true joy of life.

But Sandra felt that she needed a 'guide book' to help her in doing something new each day, to expand her mind and reconnect her with others and with nature, in celebration of this wonderful gift of life. But there wasn't one... so she wrote it!

In these pages you will find nearly two hundred suggestions for activities, some brief and others deeper, which are sure to lift your spirits and give you a lighter step on your journey. One or two of them may even change your life entirely...

Ten per cent of this book's royalties will be donated to the National Animal Welfare Trust, to help them continue their marvellous work with animals.

Notes from the Author

This book is written for anyone who feels that the joy of life has disappeared. Many of us have been shaken by a life-changing event, or simply lost our direction. If our precious lives are to be meaningful, then such challenges can be seen as 'blessings in disguise', catalysts for change. So here are nearly two hundred spiritual and holistic ideas to be used as a reservoir of insights and activities, any one of which may gently push us into new ways of learning and living. Gradually, life can be transformed from a glass-half-empty to one that is full to overflowing.

You may dip into this book at any point, but quite a few of the suggestions are specific to their dates of entry so it may be a good idea to check a little way ahead. Feel free simply to ignore any suggestions that do not resonate with you – but please don't be afraid to move out of your comfort zone occasionally!

Now, I do not wish to offend any religious or other belief practices so throughout this book I have used words such as God or the Source to refer to the divinity within or higher power beyond us all. I do not follow any one particular faith myself and respect others' ways. But I do believe that everything is energy, so if our hearts and minds are open, loving and kind, then the energy around us – and attracted to us – will be of similar vibrations. That is the spirit of this book.

Grounding and Protection

When adopting any new spiritual practice such as the suggestions offered here, it is important to feel grounded and protected, staying in the present and maintaining a good energetic vibration. For some, protection may involve prayers to God, calling in spirit guides or invoking guardians of the four directions, to name a few practices. There are other suggestions in the entry for the 11th of January. We also need to know that our body is safe and in a safe environment, so cleansing the space where we meditate or conduct any charm work, for example, is important; this can be done by smudging, sound healing or spraying holy water into the corners of the home.

May you rediscover, as I have, your own days of Heaven!

Contents

January

In the northern hemisphere we remain in deep winter and the Crone goddess still reigns. It is a time for continued inner reflection and contemplation, along with some preparations for our journey into this new year. It is time for a new cycle, new resolutions and new plans. Although in the dark of the year still, there is usually evidence of a tiny glimmer of lighter evenings on their way. Snowdrops and early daffodils peep through the cold ground with the promise of nature's rekindling.

1ˢᵗ January – Blessing

Pierre Pradervand's wonderful book *The Gentle Art of Blessing* encourages us to practise blessing others as he believes it "opens an inner font of healing and bliss which grows with every blessing." When attempting to bless others in heartfelt ways, as if kind thoughts and feelings are being poured from our hearts, it is possible for us to acknowledge our own grateful thanks for being alive in a wonderful life and wishing this for others too.

These genuine wishes for others to receive blessings, whether from ourselves or petitioning blessings for them from the deities of our personal faiths and beliefs, can engender within us a sense of stillness and peace, being mindful of our connectedness and our kindred spirit with all upon Mother Earth.

Whether we bless or request blessings for individual strangers at random, those appearing to be in poor health, young children with their lives ahead of them or groups and families, this practice is now a tiny seed of thought in our minds to consider cultivating at the beginning of a new year.

Blessing others is a private matter and not an overt activity and could be considered as a silent prayerful request to God or Source to intervene with light and healing.

Helpful tip: Reading Pierre Pradervand's book can greatly assist us in understanding how to make blessing a daily routine.

3ʳᵈ January – The Quadrantids Meteor Shower

The first annual family of meteor showers best seen in the night sky in the northern hemisphere are the Quadrantids; their peak dates are 3ʳᵈ and 4ᵗʰ January, although they range between the 28ᵗʰ of December and the 12ᵗʰ of January. The easiest way to describe where to look in the night sky today is to look up and find the Plough. Once done, look to the left a little and this is where the Quadrantids will hail from (the constellation system of Bootes). On a good night it is possible to see up to a hundred meteors.

Dress up in warm clothing tonight and sit on a chair allowing easy viewing of the night sky. When a meteor is seen, say a wish. Have a lot of wishes ready! Wishes could be for good health for yourself, your family and friends but let's also make wishes for all those on the Earth who are suffering. Be adventurous in your wishes for humankind and don't forget to extend it to animals and nature, as many meteors may be seen in this particular shower.

Helpful tip: For those in large towns and cities with light pollution, try finding an area where the night sky is visible and arrange a small party with like-minded friends, taking flasks of hot chocolate to help keep warm!

5th January – The Goddess Ukemochi

Ukemochi is the Shinto goddess of food. This is a good day to be grateful for the food and sustenance in our lives and to express this with a prayer of thanks and, if able, to donate some food to the local food bank or other aid agency providing for those in need.

This is also an opportunity for us carefully to consider our choices in the food we eat or prepare for others in terms of its nutritional values and whether we receive its full benefit when we cook or prepare it. Let's consider whether we sometimes dishonour food and where it came from simply by wasting it unnecessarily; this is just as applicable to our domestic situations as to organisations where excess food is considered a waste product.

This is the start of a new year and perhaps an opportunity to begin eating more healthily. Call upon the goddess Ukemochi for her guidance in making appropriate choices.

Helpful tip: The energies from a moonstone crystal can help us with nutrient absorption from our food by placing one over the intestinal area for approximately fifteen minutes.

7th January – The Ethiopian Christmas

Ethiopian Christians celebrate Christmas on this day. Ethiopia is one of the oldest nations of Africa and it is said that one of the three magi seeking the baby Jesus was from here. The St Mary of Zion cathedral in Aksum claims to house the Ark of the Covenant, which contains the tablets of stone upon which the Ten Commandments were inscribed.

As the Ten Commandments were basic guidelines for people to live by, let us spend a short while today reflecting upon the guidance we have received in our lives – from our parents, siblings, friends, teachers and work colleagues. Let's acknowledge and appreciate the good guidance we received (and learn from any poor guidance!) so we can grow from it.

Then we may reflect upon the guidance we have offered to others and how doing so can be a huge responsibility; it can bring about life-enhancing learning for the recipient on the one hand but a springboard to all sorts of unnecessary turbulence for them on the other. We should question whether our guidance came from our set beliefs or whether it arose from innovative thinking outside the box, using our wisdom and accessing our intuitive nature. Has any of our guidance been flawed for whatever reason? Has our guidance stemmed from a desire to be of service to others? Has it stemmed from our own value systems and, if so, we should consider that our value system may be vastly different to those held by others and it is important to be mindful about imposing our values upon them. Consider the external and internal influences that informed our guidance, which may have come from an empirical approach or may have arisen as a kneejerk reaction.

After some reflection, let's intend that when we offer guidance to others in the future it comes from a place of wellness and compassion in the heart and mind, as guidance can be of such value when provided from this peaceful place. One only has to think of Mahatma Gandhi to bring awareness of this to the fore.

Helpful tip: When reflecting on such things, hold a piece of rose quartz crystal, the energy of which helps us to find compassion in our hearts; after all, old memories may need to be released with compassion.

9ᵗʰ January – Archangel Gabriel

One of the colours associated with Archangel Gabriel is pure white. He is often depicted holding white lilies, for purity, in old paintings when giving the news to Mary of the impending birth of Jesus. Archangel Gabriel is a messenger and can assist us on our life's journey, helping us in our communication with others and with our inner selves, to nurture our soul and spirit.

Today, set time aside to meditate with the specific intention of asking Archangel Gabriel to inspire us with his gifts of purity and compassionate communication and with developing intuition. Having prepared ourselves, we imagine ourselves in a bubble of an incredibly bright and pure white light, enveloping the whole of the physical body and infusing the energy fields with soothing caresses. We visualise the light spreading throughout our internal body, shining upon and through our organs, blood, muscles and skeletal structure so the whole of the body is infused with pure, divine light.

Then we visualise this bright light swirling through our energy fields, cleansing and soothing and re-energising them. Stay with this visualisation for around five minutes and at the end of the meditation thank Archangel Gabriel for his love and guidance.

Helpful tip: While meditating, perhaps hold a snow quartz or selenite crystal to help with visualising the bright light. Snow quartz can assist us with linking to our inner wisdom and intuition, and selenite helps with calmness and peace during meditation.

11ᵗʰ January – Grounding and Protection

Protection for ourselves, our families, our homes, cars and pets is an important action to consider each day depending upon what is happening in our lives. Here are some suggestions to consider for grounding and protection routines.

Visualise yourself under a brilliant white archway of light. If heading into a difficult situation, or planning to be around others who can deplete your energies, draw up a purple cloak from Mother Earth, draping it around your shoulders and all around your body, pulling the hood up over your head. Then visualise mirrors upon the purple cloak that deflect negative energy but allow in positive and loving vibrational energies.

We may think of the energy field in the shape of an egg and being of camouflage, so that our presence is unnoticed by others when we walk through some areas. Alternatively, we could think of a bubble coloured to whatever suits our need at the time, adding a prayer requesting protection from Archangel Michael. When going on long car journeys, let's visualise the car and everyone in it being surrounded by a huge blue bubble with an angel on the roof!

During meditation, grounding is important for us and the following may be used as a basis or something to be expanded upon. Imagine small roots growing out from the soles of the feet, where there are mini 'chakras' or energy centres. These roots travel swiftly down into the earth through the soil, crystals and minerals until they reach a huge cave lit up with the orange glow of the Earth's core; here there is a large haematite crystal, offering good grounding energies.

Wrap your roots around the haematite and allow its energies to travel back up the roots and into your feet and on up through the whole of the body. The colour of haematite's energies flowing throughout the body can be visualised as red, which is the colour of strength and courage.

When offering healing to others, as well as the above grounding routine it is important that one's own energies are not depleted. Imagine your crown chakra, at the top of the head, opening like a crystal lotus flower, its petals opening one by one and sending out tiny fibre-optic tendrils up into the universe to link with divine energies. The loving, healing and protecting energies of the divine then travel down the tendrils into your crown and throughout your body. The colours of this energy are a mixture of gold, silver, bronze and violet, which glitters and swirls as it mixes with the grounding red. When breathing, visualise these colours being expelled to form a surrounding bubble of protection.

When we finish any meditation or healing practices, it is then important to close down our chakras by allowing the roots to release from the haematite crystal and wind their way back into the soles of our feet and then close over the bottom of each foot with a golden disc of light. For the crown chakra, release the fibre-optic tendrils from the divine source and draw them back in, visualising the crystal petals of the lotus flower closing one by one, then place a golden disc of light over this chakra too.

Our solar plexus energy centre is an important chakra for our emotions. Even if not deliberately opening this energy centre during meditation or healing, it would be worthwhile visualising a golden disc over this centre too with a mirror facing outwards to deflect any harm so that our emotional energies are not leached. In everyday life, we often instinctively cover this area with our arms when we feel emotionally threatened.

Helpful tip: Placing a haematite crystal nearby ready to hold for grounding after a meditation could be beneficial, or you may prefer to place the feet upon one or two of these very grounding crystals throughout.

13ᵗʰ January – Old Norse Winter Nights

In olden days, in this period of the year thoughts focused upon the crops being planned. With the ancients' practices of honouring gods and goddesses, and acknowledging the harmony of living in community with nature and the spirits of the land, offerings would have been made in advance to prepare the soil.

The Old Norse Winter Nights, a period of thirteen days, was when offerings were made to the Norse gods Thor and Freyr to ensure a good growth season for the crops in order to provide sustenance for the following winter.

This is also a time for us to consider our plans and aspirations. Are they linked with the land, our family, our work or our home? We contemplate how happiness would feel for us at the fruition of our plans by the end of this year and, when doing so, we think of who or what may have helped to bring our plans about and how these grateful thoughts would feel.

Let's spend a few moments trying tangibly to feel these thoughts and senses within our body and then consider how these grateful thoughts could be expressed. Would it be by pouring a little drop of wine upon the roots of a tree, perhaps, or by donating clothes to a charity? Would it be by offering to shop for an elderly neighbour or walking the dog for a sick friend?

This is not behaving with a pay-off mentality, it is recognising and acknowledging that by helping and working with others, and living with the natural flow of the universe, we create a feeling of honour and respect for the care and nurture of Mother Earth and all living on her. It is similar to our ancestors honouring the spirits of the land.

15ᵗʰ January – A Quick Wealth Charm

A quick and easy charm to ensure continuing wealth is to secrete a £2 or €2 coin, or two $1 coins, together with a small quartz crystal under the entrance mat. When doing so, we thank the universe for the abundance in our life and request that it continues. This is not meant for greed but for ongoing needs in life, to pay our way without worry and concern. Don't forget, too, that when we are flush we should consider sharing some of our good fortune with others.

According to numerology, the number two has the energy of wishing for a partner and when combined with the amplifying energy of the quartz crystal there is added encouragement for increased finance.

Helpful tip: In preparing for this or similar charms, cleanse coins of the energies of all those who have previously handled them by placing them in sea salt for an hour.

17ᵗʰ January – The Hindu Mother Aditi

Mother Aditi is known to Hindus as the Mother of the Gods and she is petitioned for protection and nourishment. They seek her help also for a smooth path in life. We have incarnated on Earth to experience life and, although we all need to face challenges from time to time to help us in our growth and to learn resilience along the way, a continuous barrage of problems and obstacles can simply become too much. It can stunt our lives and our evolutionary path becomes side-lined.

When these moments arise, petition help from Mother Aditi for her aid in finding a smoother path or course of action. Indeed, we could think of something today for which her inspiration would be much appreciated: it could perhaps be a project being worked on where things are not going according to plan. Request Mother Aditi's inspiration and be open to options arising that provide valuable insights and can be taken advantage of; they may just be exactly what is needed to enable forward movement again.

19th January – Black Pepper Essential Oil

Black pepper essential oil is purported to have protective properties and is used by many for this purpose. Today, purchase a small bottle of black pepper essential oil and every now and again pour three drops onto the front doormat so that whoever steps on it when entering your home will have any negative energies deflected before they enter.

This includes ourselves, for times when we are around people who can be emotionally draining or who may unknowingly thrive on creating difficult circumstances. We don't want their energy hanging around us. Black pepper essential oil can also be used to offer protection around the workplace door, if regularly visited by stressed colleagues who perhaps have become 'energy vampires'!

21st January – The Feast of Hecate

This deity, pronounced 'Hecketty', was the grand-daughter of two sibling Titans, Koios and Phoibe, and early Greek myth states that she was a powerful goddess who could bring many blessings of wealth and success. She is known as the Queen of Witches and Magic and the 20th to the 21st of January is marked as her feast.

Hecate is often depicted near a fork in the road, denoting a path less travelled that provides opportunities for transformation to be found when facing challenges or another path where life may be easier but provides little opportunity for growth. Some Tarot readers will use the Crossroads Spread in divination to assist in highlighting the potential emotional and logical influences surrounding a decision, in order to seek better insight and understanding.

Today, we could light a candle and sprinkle the herb rosemary in a circle around its base, requesting Hecate's guidance. We shall then spend a little time in peace and think about any blocks in our life or any choices or decisions to be made on our journey, so that old notions and frameworks cease being an impediment and instead we can make decisions that engender improvement.

Intuitive insights into our choices or dilemmas may arise during meditation or later in a dream. They can also just pop into the mind while going about our routine day during the following week. Then we could thank Hecate for her guidance by planting some rosemary in the garden or a windowsill pot in the coming weeks.

Helpful tip: Azurite crystal can bring clearer understanding of our choices and decisions. Also, if you own a Tarot pack, try the Crossroads Spread for a specific matter to be considered in order to enable deeper insight, as the symbolic imagery of the cards and their meanings may give a new perception of the matter. This can help us to listen to our inner selves and to understand any emotional issues not previously acknowledged, freeing us to become aware of a new direction.

23rd January – The Goddess Artemis

In Greek myth, Artemis is the twin sister of Apollo and cousin to Hecate. Artemis was a strong goddess, able to stand up for herself and one who loved all nature. (It should be recognised, however, that there's polarity in the myths of the Greek pantheon of gods and goddesses, in that they also murdered, plundered and killed for sport...) She was considered to be the goddess to call upon when inner strength and self-confidence was required.

The fir tree was sacred to Artemis so at this time we can prepare for a future when our inner strength will be needed by sourcing a fir tree and planting it in the garden. Alternatively we could plant one in a suitably sized container that can be brought into the home at Christmas to be decorated and then placed outside again afterwards. If you don't have a garden, 'adopt' a fir tree somewhere special for you in nature.

Once the fir tree has been sourced and planted, put a moonstone crystal in the earth nearby, since moonstone was considered sacred to Artemis. This tree is now a natural 'altar place' to sit near when requiring inner strength.

As Artemis was called the Goddess of the Hunt, and among the animals sacred to her was the dog, let's take this further and associate the sacred link to dogs with Sirius in Canis Major. In the northern hemisphere, Sirius is the brightest star in the sky when looking south and is best seen during the evenings from December to February.

Therefore, during the dark winter evenings of January when we still await the first stirrings of spring life, let's be near our fir tree altar and visualise Sirius showering the strength of its bright light upon us and the confidence of Artemis flowing around us, suffusing our energy fields with confidence and mental strength.

Helpful tip: Holding a moonstone in partnership with the moonstone buried near the fir tree may help in calming any jittery emotions and enable an understanding that life moves in cycles, just as in nature. When doing so, make an intention for a new cycle of confidence and mental strength to begin.

25th January – "It's all out there waiting for you."

Captain James T Kirk of the Starship Enterprise said the above words in the original television series of Star Trek, and it's true! It is all out there waiting for us all. Life is to be lived.

We should try to wake up each day in wonder at what is possible. What fun awaits us? What excitement awaits us? What learning and understanding will we gain today? What part of life's experience on this planet that we wish to achieve on our journey is about to unfold? Will we love today? Will we cry today? Will we laugh today? So many possibilities…

If travelling to work, for example, a different route today might change our lives. Let us not block the flow of life's abundance. Let us be open and receptive to the wonders and mysteries. Let us not become bored with life. There is so much waiting for us to discover and there's a beautiful planet to live on while making those discoveries. Let us marvel at the spectacular sunrises and sunsets and be amazed at the ever-changing seascapes.

Let us become genuinely grateful for everything – even our difficulties, for these are milestones of learning and growth with potential breakthroughs allowing us to escape from our fixed assumptions and old fears. Let us step into the world with new eyes, as changing attitudes to our challenges can naturally encourage forward movement.

If our sense of purpose is a little lost, then let us try following our passion and allow the universe to be the benevolent energetic force that it is. Explore the universe with all it brings into our lives, because it is "all out there waiting for you."

27th January – A Meditation Group

Although it is recommended to meditate regularly every day, for some, starting out like this can become too onerous and then the practice ceases. To assist with meditating regularly, consider joining a meditation group. There are many different types of meditation practice and not all may be suitable but some will; on the other hand, the many types may suit your personality in terms of variety being the spice of life.

A meditation group will often allow for several types and styles of meditation, of varying lengths of time. If new to meditation or looking to expand your current practice, then perhaps this is something to be explored. If you are unable to find a suitable group, but a few of your like-minded friends are interested in taking this further, you could consider creating your own meditation group. This can be held within your own home, where friendship bonding and support play an important role in the rhythm of our lives.

Helpful tip: Hatha yoga is a gentle form, involving some meditative practice within its positions, known as asanas; this may be an introduction to meditation whilst obtaining the benefits of yoga at the same time.

29th January – Prayers of Gratitude

Rhonda Byrne, author of *The Secret*, is a keen exponent of 'thank you prayers', or prayers of gratitude, and in her book *The Magic* she recommends writing a gratitude list each day for a certain period as an example of realising just how much there is to be thankful for in our lives. Being thankful for turning on a tap for clean water, for flicking a switch to obtain instant light or heating, for our families and friends, our homes, cars, pets, jobs and food are some of the usual reasons for gratefulness in our lives.

However, on retiring to bed each night, how about considering the day's events and expressing gratitude for the achievements, the learning, the laughter and so on? From today, let's try to give regular thank you prayers; they can be simple or elaborate and at whatever time is suitable, perhaps even a special monthly event on each full moon.

We have so much in our lives and so many opportunities and choices available to us. Thanking God, or the Creator, or Source, the angels or the universe, is a positive energy being expressed and sent out to the universe. If expressed from the heart with genuine gratitude, it is a pure and loving energy. Just think of the amount of pure and loving energy we can all generate for the universe simply by regularly stating our heartfelt thanks through gratitude prayers.

31st January – Amethyst, the Aquarius Crystal

There are several crystals associated with each of the twelve astrological signs and for Aquarius there's amethyst, due to its many qualities as an all-round healing stone and as an aid for life's journey by enhancing our spiritual awareness. It also helps meditation with its tranquillity.

Many crystal books highly recommend amethyst as essential for those starting out on their crystal journey and also for lightworkers. Its energies protect our auric fields, its spiritual qualities guide our intuition especially when healing, and its beautiful colour reminds us of the Violet Flame of Transformation, linked with Archangel Zadkiel, Lord Hilarion and the Angel of St Germaine.

You might research the amethyst today and buy one if possible (a tumble stone is very cheap). Then try working with it by holding it each day and visualising its colour washing over the body, or by holding it during meditation when seeking inspiration.

February

We are stepping into the period of the Maiden Goddess. This can very often be the coldest month in the northern hemisphere with snowfall and yet we also have small signs of life stirring such as the snowdrop and crocus. Like these early flowers our plans, following inner reflection during the dark months, can also start to stir and show signs of future blossoming.

1st February – Imbolc

On this day is celebrated Imbolc, pronounced 'Immok', and it is a day to visit a holy well. When doing so, it's a good idea to collect some of the water in a glass container and use it at home, for example to anoint our candles for added potency when we send wishes of love and healing to others. If you are visiting a holy well today, it may well have been 'dressed' for Imbolc with greenery and flowers. Offer thanks to the holy well, too, by scattering some indigenous white flower seeds around the area or by planting snowdrops or lily of the valley.

Brighid or Bride, pronounced as 'Breed', is a Celtic goddess and is associated with Imbolc and healing or holy wells. Brighid is also known as the Irish Fire Goddess. As the midwife of spring, she represents the birth of spring time, new lambs and ewe's milk, hence the white colour of the flowers. This is a time of rejuvenation and early signs of fertility returning to Mother Earth. Interestingly, Archangel Gabriel is linked with this period of time and the colour associated with him is also white.

It is worth bearing in mind that, sadly, hundreds of these ancient wells have fallen into disrepair, become stagnant or even disappeared altogether. Please therefore ensure that any water you collect is clean and will not become a health hazard. You may like to consider, if you have experienced a pleasant time at the sacred well, finding out if there are any local organisations trying to ensure that these historic sites are properly maintained for our future generations. If their activities are of interest, you might join in with them in some way. Here are some British holy wells that could be explored:

Madron Wishing Well, and nearby baptistery within an ancient
   Pagan-Christian building, near Penzance, Cornwall.
St Austin's Well, Cerne Abbas, Dorset.
Upwey Wishing Well, Dorset.
Well and shrine to St Tibba and St Ebba at Ryhall, Rutland.

Holy Well at St John the Baptist Church, Needingworth in
  Cambridgeshire.
Holy Well of St Mary the Virgin at Dunsford, Surrey.
Black Prince's Well at Harbledown, near Canterbury in Kent.
Sugar Well at Meanwood, Leeds, Yorkshire.
Holy Well at King's Newton in Derbyshire.
St Cuthbert's Well in Durham.
St Brighid's Well, Kildare, Ireland.
St Seriol's Well, Penmon, Anglesey, Wales.
St Non's Well, St David's, Pembrokeshire, Wales.
St Mary's Well, Culloden, near Inverness in Scotland.
Burghead Well between Lossiemouth and Findhorn in Morayshire,
  Scotland.

Helpful tip: A bedtime drink of warm milk sprinkled with comforting
cinnamon and nutmeg may encourage feelings of being supported
and cocooned in love. This is similar to how Mother Earth has offered
her love and support to nature, cocooned in stillness over the winter
and now being ready to awaken to the light.

3rd February – Gridding with Crystals

Gridding the whole of our home, including the garden, is an easy
way to create a haven or sanctuary of peace and also to protect the
home if this is relevant. Not only is it possible to grid the home, each
room can be gridded as well. If a child suffers from nightmares or
a baby frets greatly at night, gridding the bed or cot with a loving
crystal energy such as rose quartz could be considered. In this case,
keep things safe by placing any crystals under the mattress or the
bed, where small hands can't reach them.

Gridding is easy to do and, if choosing a crystal such as rose
quartz which is in plentiful supply and relatively inexpensive to buy,

there will be minimal outlay. All that's necessary is to place a crystal in the corner of each room, ensuring that no pets or children can swallow them, and allow their energies to work. Before gridding, cleanse the crystals and then set your intention with them by holding and speaking to them. This can be as simple as saying, "Please use your energies to bring love and harmony into my home." Another example of gridding is to place a black obsidian or black tourmaline crystal on the ledge at the top of the door frame of each room of the home. These crystals soak up negative energies; however, they will need cleansing regularly.

Each week – perhaps best on a Saturday, which is linked with the planet Saturn and good for overcoming obstacles – place each crystal under a running tap and envision any negative energies collected by the crystal being released and going down the drain, leaving the crystal cleansed and ready to work again. Other forms of cleansing are placing the crystal in sea salt, dried lavender or organic brown rice for several hours. If this cleansing is completed in the morning then the crystals can be left on a windowsill for the remainder of the day to re-energise with the sun's power. If the moon is in a full phase, then charging crystals with the moon's energy may be preferred.

If you wish to grid the whole of your home and garden then bury the crystals in the ground. Set your intention and add the request for Mother Earth to keep them cleansed and energised so they can remain in situ. If protection is also required then add a crystal such as black obsidian. To strengthen this further by 'the power of three', add a clear quartz crystal to amplify the energies of the rose quartz and black obsidian.

Helpful tip: Selenite is a lovely stone for gridding too, due to its energies of creating a safe and quiet space; if gridding a room for meditation or healing then this may be the perfect choice. However, selenite is a crystal that should not be immersed in water.

5th February – A Metaphysical Book Club

Reading is a favourite pastime for many and with so much choice available to guide us on our journeys we could easily run out of room in our homes! Today you could consider starting a metaphysical book club with some like-minded friends. This can help us in our everyday interactions by simply swapping books, sharing opinions and views on what has been learned and what is planned to take forward. The additional learning gained from our peers' different perceptions can prove to be of great value. And stimulating conversations can bring about winds of change, encouraging us to expand our horizons and rewrite old patterns that no longer reflect how we wish to conduct ourselves.

A bonus of being a member of a book club is that many of us create our own wish-lists of books to buy or borrow when we're able to, and the club can help us achieve our wish-lists expeditiously and cheaply.

Book meetings can take place in our homes on a rotational basis. If there are several people who would like to be included, perhaps a local bookshop would be interested in hosting an area for this to take place as there's the bonus for them of possibly selling books to members of the group. Some supermarket cafes and libraries also set aside community space for meetings free of charge.

Helpful tip: If starting a metaphysical book club, the following three books offer a broad range of ideas that would prove very interesting for a new group to read and then discuss: *Aura Child* by A I Kaymen about the experiences of an Indigo child, *Tap Once for Yes* by Jacquie Parton, describing contact with her son in the spirit world, and *Can You Hear Me?* by Janine Wilbraham who writes about animal communication.

7th February – Julian of Norwich

This lady was an English anchoress living in Norwich in the Middle Ages who became one of the most important of all English mystics, writing the first book by a woman in the English language, called *Revelations of Divine Love.* An anchoress is a religious woman who lives a reclusive life in a simple, single cell, usually attached to the wall of a church. She has been called Julian of Norwich, her true name being unknown, after the church of St Julian's that her anchorage was attached to.

Her visions of God in May, 1373, form the basis of her book in which she described God as merciful and enfolding us in unconditional love. Within the book she mentions a response from God to one of her questions as, "…all shall be well, and all shall be well, and all manner of things shall be well." This has been considered as probably the first affirmation or mantra to be written in the English language.

You may like to research Julian of Norwich today and perhaps download her book from the Internet (see the Bibliography).

Helpful tip: In Transcendental Meditation (also known as TM and taught by the Indian guru Maharishi Mahesh Yogi in the 1950s), continuous and silent repetition of a personal mantra for approximately twenty minutes each morning and night is said to be of much benefit for us. Perhaps, then, adopting the above affirmation, being 'offered from God', as our own silent mantra is another option for us to bring peace and good health into our lives.

9th February – Oracle Cards

Gosh, which set to choose? There are hundreds of them ranging in size, cost and styles. If your preference is to work with angels then focus on choosing an angel oracle set of cards. Likewise for animals, dolphins, mermaids and so on. Oracle cards are uplifting and help to reinforce positive aspects of everyday life, encouraging us to be mindful of being and feeling positive.

A good many oracle packs have a little booklet that suggests various layouts to try, although many people just choose one randomly each day. Whatever deck is chosen, enjoy them and be happy in your use of them.

Helpful tip: If you already have several oracle packs, try shuffling each pack and then picking one card from each. It may be surprising that the same theme arises from the different decks. When this occurs, take note as it could be the universe's way of drawing your attention to something important.

11ᵗʰ February – The Mind Body Spirit Festival

MBS festivals or fayres are many and varied from local town and village halls to national and international events with renowned guest speakers. These fayres are marvellous opportunities to view, explore and liaise with various people about the modalities of healing and spirituality they practise.

Some people find that these MBS fayres have an atmosphere different to any other public events due to the many spiritual practices exhibited, and mingled with these wonderful energies are hundreds of crystals for sale with their own subtle vibrations enabling us to feel uplifted. Not only are the varied stalls of interest, there are usually workshops to attend or taster sessions on offer for several therapies at reasonable prices.

So today, check out your local area to see which MBS fayres are planned in the forthcoming weeks and make plans to pay a visit. Or why not try one of the national or international events, perhaps getting together with some like-minded friends and arranging a special trip to the most appealing festival?

13th February – Violet, the February Birth Flower

The sweet violet, which the Victorians adored and planted many of in their gardens, is not a common flower now and yet its flowering times are perhaps when colour is required most in our gardens, in February and again in the autumn.

The descriptive phrase 'a shrinking violet', assigned to shy and oversensitive people who prefer to remain in the background, has long been used. Sensitivity towards others can inform our compassionate nature and is therefore an important aspect of our characters. However, oversensitivity can be detrimental by creating distress and disease in ourselves, causing us to shrink away from contact with others. But in the language of flowers it is felt that violets offer the opposite effect, in that they encourage us to come out of our shells, become more positive and confident and not to be afraid of failures since they can help us to learn on our life's journey. The energy of violets is also thought to offer psychic protection for those working with healing and spirit communication.

Today, source some violets ready to plant and, when admiring their delicacy, think about how confidence can be achieved on your journey whilst still maintaining a healthy sensitivity. This is about freeing ourselves from any inner default settings when our sensitivity works in overdrive, and contemplating how we can satisfy our inner spirit for our highest and greatest good.

Helpful tip: Citrine and aragonite crystals can help with decreasing oversensitivity.

15th February – The Japanese Buddhist Goddess Benzaiten

Benzaiten is a goddess of all things that flow, such as music, speech or water, as well as being a protector deity and goddess of eloquence. From today, let us monitor our speech in terms of swearing, blaspheming or moaning and complaining and being derogatory about others. Let us monitor whether our conversations contain too much pessimism and negativity; if this is so, it potentially leads to us making these low vibrations the focus of our energies, thus attracting more of the same.

If on reflection we realise that we are somewhat guilty of the above, then let us petition this goddess of eloquence for help so that we can start changing the lower verbal vibration emanating from the throat chakra to a higher vibration, by speaking more eloquently and gently. Let us become more uplifting with our words, having kinder and more honourable conversations in all of our interactions – and call upon this goddess when we need to speak with inspiration.

It may be helpful to place a simple reminder of Benzaiten's wonderful energies on the fridge door as a clarion call to read each day for a month. This could reinforce our moral compass in speaking kindly and may motivate us in blazing a new trail with our work colleagues as well as with our families.

Helpful tip: Wearing a blue scarf, blue necklace or a blue tie helps to balance the energies of the throat chakra and may enable changes in conversation to a more gentle vibration. Blue helps to clear stuck energies and allows us to converse with others with added integrity and authenticity.

17ᵗʰ February – The Roman Goddess Juno

This ancient deity, sometimes called Juno Moneta, was married to Jupiter and considered to be queen of the Roman pantheon of gods. Coins minted near her temple in ancient Rome, which was protected by geese, displayed the head of Juno struck on one side; some also considered Juno Moneta as a guardian of finances.

Linking with the theme of geese protecting Juno's temple, source a goose feather today to place in your purse or wallet or with your business accounts. When doing so, respectfully ask the goddess Juno to offer her protection for your finances. Another option is to place one in the 'wealth corner' of your home.

Helpful tip: If feeling artistic, try additional symbolic empowerments such as decorating the goose feather using acrylic paint with symbols of good luck such as a horseshoe, a four-leaf clover or perhaps a £, € or $ sign. Another option would be to use a rune symbol such as Fehu, which is linked with prosperity.

19th February – The Wolf
(American Animal Sign, 19th Feb – 20th Mar)

While receiving a crystal healing in one particular session several years ago, I went quite deeply into a meditation and in that state saw a wolf appear and approach me. This lone wolf stood steadfast, looking piercingly at me with such dignity. It was nothing to be fearful of and I welcomed its presence. This wolf appeared for me at a time when I was on a path of being single, my marriage having just broken down, so Wolf reminded and encouraged me that I had the inner fortitude to live a full life and that I could approach difficulties with dignity and bravery.

Wolf appeared again a couple of years later when, in another meditation, I was confronted by a raging black bull, pawing at the ground (which reflected a problem I was experiencing). I was unable to move with the bull drawing closer but then, appearing from my left side, came Wolf to offer steadfast protection and guidance.

I can still easily recall and visualise this wolf perfectly in my meditations and now know that when life becomes a little tough at times I can look to my inner strength to help me through. I have since learned that the wolf is my 'gatekeeper' in psychic work.

For yourself today, visualise a wolf travelling in the wilderness with loping gait, exhibiting stamina, inner fortitude, fearlessness and bravery. When in a pack, wolves have structure and leadership, with the teaching and nurture of their young in mind for their survival. The lone wolf, although without pack structure support, also exhibits inner fortitude. The lone wolf may also be seen as a pathfinder and if we're feeling slightly strayed or becoming distracted on our life's journey then Wolf may be able to assist in re-igniting and rekindling our sense of purpose.

Let's research and question what can be adopted from Wolf's qualities and be ready to call on him in the future when we need inner strength, or some solitude for learning, or with guidance in finding our path again.

21ˢᵗ February – Tiger Iron, the Pisces Crystal

Tiger iron is a banded crystal with layers incorporating the three other crystals of tiger's eye, red jasper and haematite. These are quite powerful crystals in themselves, so three-in-one creates a power-house gem! Tiger iron is particularly associated with Pisces; however, it is useful for our journey as it helps us to maintain grounding and balance.

It is a stone of strength, stamina and courage. When actions in life require these attributes, there may still be times when an array of mixed emotions, thoughts and beliefs create chaotic feelings; this is where tiger iron can act with its stabilising energies.

One way of using tiger iron is while meditating, when it can easily rest in one's lap and act as the grounding anchor, especially if the intention is to go deep into one's psyche. Research tiger iron today and check out its qualities to see if they will be of use on your journey.

23rd **February – The Moon**

The Moon major arcana card in the Tarot is linked with Pisces. The moon as viewed from Earth is forever changing: growing, evolving, fulfilling and then waning to disappear. Then also the Moon goddess for witches is known as the Triple Goddess of maiden-mother-crone; in its first phase it is the young maiden growing and learning about life, then in its full moon phase we have the mother and the fulfilment of family life, and in its waning phase we have the crone who has achieved and learned much, with knowledge and wisdom to share, but who is growing old and nearing her time to pass.

Thus human life is similar to the moon's phases. We evolve and grow all the time with phases and cycles in life. It is good to experience and embrace life in these cycles by making the most of them so that we can gain wisdom, which in turn informs our continuing journey. The often quoted phrase, 'this time too shall pass', is very relevant as life does evolve, does change, does ebb and flow and it would be beneficial for us to evolve and change and grow also instead of remaining stuck and perhaps sabotaging ourselves when opportunities arise for us to transform.

Consider the older generation, the crones. Think about the wisdom, knowledge and experience they have accrued through the various phases and cycles of their lives and the conditions that the social burdening of various nations has placed on them. For the fortunate ones, growing up in family homes of three generations, daily conversations and interactions took place that helped to enrich their lives as love and mutual respect enabled expression of thoughts, feelings and concerns in an authentic manner within a safe family environment.

So today, let's consider what can be learned from our older generations, our crones, and be grateful to them for passing on their wisdom and knowledge to us. Let's also try being grateful for the learning experienced in the phases and cycles of our own lives, whether maiden, mother or crone (or the masculine equivalents of boy, father and elder), and resolve that throughout any of these cycles we continue embracing opportunities and learning along our pathway. For this is why we have incarnated.

25ᵗʰ February – Archangel Raphael

The colour green is associated with Archangel Raphael, who is often the focus of a prayerful request to intervene with his green healing light for someone in need. Green is also a balancing colour, so Raphael can help a person to find emotional balance whilst coping with whatever health issues they have. Unbalanced emotions can cultivate disease in our bodies, thus further impacting on any health problem.

A meditation for today is to visualise being in a green bubble. When ready, let's imagine that all around are shrubs and trees in full green leaf with lush green grass at our feet. Visualise walking barefoot through the grass, feeling it brush gently past the ankles and soles of the feet. Touch the soft green leaves of the trees and shrubs and tell them how beautiful they look. When doing so, we feel them send tingling senses along our fingers in response.

Try to realise that as loving thoughts were sent to them, so they reciprocated. Sense the joyful feeling of this within the heart centre and, instead of gently touching the leaves, this time cup them in a caress and send loving thanks for providing their beauty and nourishment to our lives. In response, their tingling becomes much stronger and travels throughout our body, along with the tingling travelling from the grass up the feet and legs.

The love of our intention forms a cycle of love with nature and our green-coloured heart centres are the pivotal point of all this activity. We recognise that the more love we all send out, the more love we all receive. We can feel that love healing every part of our body and spread out to every part of the world and all in it. When finished, we should thank Archangel Raphael and the Earth with her spiritual inhabitants for cycling the green light of healing.

27th February – Tapping

EFT, the Emotional Freedom Technique, is a form of psychological acupuncture for emotional healing. It is attractive to many with its affirmation-type wording and the use of gentle tapping along the acupuncture points of our meridians. It is a simple approach that can be used anywhere, whether at home on our own when wishing to deal with a past problem or perhaps when we are about to face a difficult moment in life.

Examples of difficult moments could be when we are nervous about an imminent job interview or an examination, or even when at our local health centre waiting for blood tests to be taken. Being faced with traumas, whether large or small, can completely immobilise us both physically and mentally and this is where tapping can become very beneficial in our lives, with very quick results in some cases.

EFT can assist us in transforming the blocks in our everyday lives that cause us to stumble on our journey. When we become stuck or are continually stumbling because of a particular trauma, our minds can create a constant inner critic, forever conducting a war of attrition with itself. Tapping offers us the opportunity to recognise that we are fallible human beings, open to potential emotional turbulence each day to varying degrees. However, it then allows us to release the emotional drainage connected to the turbulence, enabling us to reaffirm with mind and body that life does not stop and we can reclaim ourselves and create new criteria of success.

Why not research tapping today, as offering another option for healing and aiding ourselves in many aspects of our everyday lives.

Helpful tip: Nick Ortner's book *The Tapping Solution* offers an easy introduction, enabling an understanding of tapping and its actions for self-healing.

29th February (for Leap Years!) – Leap Year Joy

Let us do something special today that makes our heart, mind, body, soul and spirit sing! If that's dancing then let's dance. If it's writing poetry then let's get our pens and paper out ready. If it's drawing then let's go into the wide outdoors and find inspiration to draw.

This is a day for us to have a little 'me time' and allow every part of us to sing in joy. On retiring to bed, reflect on the day and if it was a simply fab time then be grateful and set an intention to do it more often!

March

March welcomes the season of Lent, the spring equinox and celebration of Ostara, or Eostre, the goddess of fertility. This is a time of balance but also a time when nature promises future blossoming. There are daffodils, primroses and the wonderfully scented hyacinths. Mother Earth is quickening, there is change afoot and future potential is very visible. So it's a time for de-cluttering and detoxing with an energising resurgence, a time for us in the natural cycle to commence our own blossoming.

1ˢᵗ March – Ash Month (18ᵗʰ Feb – 17ᵗʰ Mar)

The ash tree has long been considered sacred by different cultures as a symbol of the life force. Yggdrasil, pronounced 'yidrassill', is also known as 'the world tree' in Scandinavian culture and associated with the water deities of Poseidon and Neptune, being linked to the element of water. Old superstitions believed the ash to have healing, mystical and protective powers.

Ash month is the time to allow our plans and ideas for our spiritual and personal transformation to take flight and embark upon their journeys. In old times this was a period when the winter snow and ice started to thaw and our ancestors were able to leave their secure shelters, beginning to journey once more; so we can associate this time with our own plans of travelling out into the universe.

We can join with nature today and write our requests to the universe, of our transformational plans, on a length of ribbon, here called a cloutie. When completed, we tie the ribbon to a tree, shrub or plant in the garden or in a tub so that the air element takes our requests to the universe.

There are specific coloured ribbons associated with certain desires. Red is for protection, strength, passion, courage, vitality and willpower; green is for money, fertility, growth, abundance, luck and employment; blue is for healing, patience, harmony and communication; yellow is for intellect, study, divination, friendship and creativity; gold is for happiness, success, prosperity and career matters; purple is for wisdom, spiritual love, honour, psychic ability and business.

Helpful tip: Hanging the ribbon from a well-known cloutie tree in your local area may be preferred, although this action is now becoming controversial in some places due to the sheer number of clouties potentially harming the habitat for wildlife.

3rd March – The Aquamarine Crystal

Aquamarine's several shades of blue, turquoise, jade and pale green within one crystal are so beautiful to behold and one is reminded of the spectacular blending of sea colours around the Cornish coastline and elsewhere. Aquamarine's energies can enhance our intuition when meditating and some like to wear aquamarine earrings for this reason, since the ears are near the higher chakra centres.

However, as the gentle blue shades are linked to the throat chakra, aquamarine can also help us with our communication. You might consider buying this crystal and allowing it to do its work, as its energies encourage us in speaking our truth with compassion, authenticity and integrity.

Helpful tip: If wishing to use aquamarine when meditating, and placing it in the area of the higher chakras, it is important to ensure good grounding; therefore, also holding a haematite crystal is recommended.

5th March – The Mexican Night of Witches

Around this time is the annual witchcraft convention in Mexico. It is attended by shamans, witches and healers, and also attracts many visitors who delight in observing the ceremonies and activities. Mass cleansing is carried out in one ceremony to clear negativity, so today try finding a quiet moment to have a body and auric field cleansing in a very simple way in your own home.

Prepare a bath and dissolve in it three heaped tablespoons of sea salt. Enjoy your relaxation time and visualise the sea salt permeating your auric field and cleansing your body. When you have finished, imagine all the negativity from this visualisation draining away down the plughole, leaving your body and auric field feeling cleansed. If it is only possible to shower at home then place the sea salt in a square of muslin or a cotton handkerchief and tie this in a knot so it can then be used as a salt body scrub.

Helpful tip: The pale pink Himalayan sea salt can be purchased for use in food and also for health and beauty routines, so if possible try to obtain Himalayan sea salt for this cleansing routine as many recognise its excellent purity.

7th March – Releasing Hooks

As our body and energy fields were physically cleansed two days ago with a bath or shower of sea salt, let's try cleansing our emotional bodies today. The following can be quite a strong meditation, especially if one is feeling pulled in many ways by work, family, friends and general commitments. Occasionally, the usual debris of life can become a weighty anchor, causing us to feel as if we're continuously swimming upstream. Always complete the usual pre-meditation grounding, calming and protecting exercise first.

Imagine being on a small but beautiful tropical island beach where it is perfectly safe and the sea lagoon surrounding the island is also perfectly safe. Visualise how beautiful the beach is with white sand and lush growth of plant life inland. Birds with wonderful plumage fly around freely, singing their songs in unison. The sun is shining and glistening upon the turquoise-coloured sea lagoon.

There is a small wooden rowing boat nearby and you decide to row out into the middle of the lagoon. Remember, it is perfectly safe to do so. After a short row to the centre of the lagoon, you decide to rest awhile and enjoy the gentle rocking of the boat, bringing further relaxation.

Now visualise seeing yourself as if from above, resting in the little rowing boat and in doing so notice that your energy fields take up the whole space of the boat. And all around the edges are black grappling hooks that are hooked into your energy fields. These are the energetic hooks of negative emotions from arguments, work stresses, irrational reactions, excessive commitments or unreasonable demands, and they need to be released.

So visualise yourself rising from your restful pose and picking up a grappling hook, releasing it into the sea. Allow the water energy to cleanse the hook and then see it disappear down into the sand, consumed by the Earth to cleanse it. Continue then to complete as many releases of these hooks as you feel necessary. These releases may be specific and linked to particular emotions that could be named, or perhaps just experience watching the hooks being released and trust that your higher self knows what is being let go.

After the releasing has been completed, see yourself settle back into your body in the boat and then slowly row back to the shore. Disembark from the rowing boat and sit on the sandy beach again, feeling peaceful after all that emotional work. Feel good and free in the sunshine and feel the sand in between your toes. Thank the Earth, too, for her part in cleansing your psychic hooks and, when you're ready, open your eyes and be back in the room.

Helpful tip: Holding a rose quartz crystal when conducting this meditation, for its compassionate love energies, is something to consider especially if you're releasing emotional baggage that may be deeply entrenched in your psyche. A flower essence may also be an option to take before the meditation, or have to hand some Rescue Remedy (combined flower essences) to take should a strong emotional release be felt and some calm comfort be needed.

9th March – Feng Shui

The basic concept of Feng Shui is to create harmony and balance in the home utilising colours, furniture and plant placings, bringing peace and comfort for those living there, including pets and visitors. When our homes are harmonised this has a consequent beneficial effect on us, and any spiritual practice undertaken at home such as meditation will have a head start as a certain degree of peace can already be felt.

Feng Shui also offers us 'work-arounds' if we are unable to change certain aspects of our home and outer surroundings. The practice provides guidance for the positive manifestation of abundance and auspicious experiences in our lives and in those of our children. When we adopt these, it is possible to map our progress from changes we may have made under this banner.

Why not investigate Feng Shui for yourself today and try adopting some of the recommendations?

Helpful tip: There are many Feng Shui books available and if you intend to purchase one then a book that provides clear pictures and diagrams to help in understanding the theory would be the best choice.

11th March – A Green Candle

Every Thursday, try the practice of lighting a green candle and when doing so dedicate it to Jupiter, planet of fortune, abundance and jollity. Acknowledge Jupiter for his part in the wonderful abundance he brings, expressing gratitude for his benevolence.

The colour green of the candle stems from the Wiccan belief that green is linked with prosperity and the day of Thursday is linked with Jupiter. We all need occasional boosts to our finances in order to pay our way in the world and this activity is almost like a regular 'cosmic order' each week; if carried out for genuine need and not greed, then this is a perfectly acceptable ritual.

What makes it even better is that when the universe does look after us financially, in turn we are further able to help others and thus share Jupiter's abundance. If this type of activity is appealing then buy a green candle today in preparation for next Thursday and for the one after and the one after, to keep the momentum.

Helpful tip: A large, green pillar candle will last a good time and is probably the best option. The opportunity to carve a £, $ or € sign into the candle makes for added potency. Perhaps you could also create a special verse to say when lighting it weekly.

13th March – Watching Uplifting Movies and Programmes

When we watch or listen to programmes containing arguments, malice, victimisation, shouting and screaming or much worse, our bodies can physically react to the low vibration of the programme's content. Our solar plexus energy centre is where we sense our emotions and, if becoming unbalanced, the area can become jittery and not feel at all its usual calm self in reaction to the external low vibration.

This poses the suggestion for us deliberately to watch movies and programmes that uplift us rather than the opposite. This is not to bury our heads in the sand and ignore events and current affairs that have an impact upon the world around us, but to encourage us in thinking about what we watch in terms of violence and malice and the insidious effect these can have on our lives and for our families.

Likewise, let's extend this to be mindful of what kind of music we listen to. Some radio frequencies are believed to have a negative effect upon us too. Further, if we listen to some of the lyrics in songs, then there's a double impact when they contain extreme negativity; if sung for long or loud enough, or heard often enough, they have the same impact as a life-affirming mantra except that now they have the opposite potential for creating dis-ease in our bodies.

15th March – Nike

Nike is the Greek winged goddess of victory who liked to win and represents strength and success. However, at what cost does winning arrive? Of course it is good to overcome difficulties and win through at the end of an ordeal; but perhaps a win-win outcome could be a much better prospect to be considered in some circumstances.

Today, let us take a little time to reflect upon our behaviours and characteristics when winning, whether it's an outright competition, a race, winning in a job situation or arranging an outcome to achieve our desires.

Being magnanimous towards others when coming first exhibits our regard for their efforts rather than being dismissive of them. Respecting their efforts and honouring them for being worthy competitors – and voicing these congratulatory words – could encourage them in their future endeavours. Acknowledging fellow competitors for their expertise encourages us in turn to push ourselves to achieve more.

Let's think about our behaviours both in the past and currently for a while and reflect whether a balance should be found so that we can all applaud achievers, irrelevant of what it is they have achieved. Even the apparently smallest milestone for one person can be a massive achievement for another, which equally deserves respect and acknowledgement.

17th March – St Patrick's Day

Today we celebrate the Irish patron saint St Patrick. History records that he was of Scottish descent but taken captive by the Irish and kept as a slave in his younger years. The well-known Irish Blessing is as relevant today as in yesteryear:

"May you always walk in sunshine.
May you never want for more.
May Irish angels rest their wings right beside your door."

If we all wish that for the people we meet from today, what a lot of happiness can be spread around the world! In fact, why not start with sending this verse as an email to friends today, or attach it to our Facebook pages, or if a more personal touch is preferred then write the verse and post it.

19th March – Heart-shaped Stones

Heart-shaped stones can be found at the beach or along stony riversides, so today visit or plan to visit a beach or riverside to search for heart-shaped stones, to be decorated in whichever artistic way you are able. Perhaps you could paint several outlines of the heart shape in decreasing sizes, using bright colours and glitter for added texture and sparkle.

Once decorated, the stones can be used as paperweights or placed in the garden as ornaments. They can be given as token gifts for family and friends or, as this is around the UK's date for Mothering Sunday too, a painted heart-shaped stone could be an additional gift for Mum.

This is a pleasant activity that can be undertaken with children, involving them in an activity based on compassion and love and linking this with thoughts, words and deeds coming from the heart.

21st March – The Spring Equinox

The spring equinox is a good time for a declutter of items or any clothes not worn for a while; if they are of perfectly good wear still, we could donate them to a charity so they can continue to be of service to others in need.

Decluttering is a mainstay of Feng Shui (see the entry for 9th March). Filling our homes with items, irrelevant of what they are or whether we really need them, blocks the flow of energy. This applies to visible areas as well as those wardrobes and cupboards crammed full of clothes and other things. By decluttering we can detoxify our homes and allow room for good energy to flow into and around them; and by donating good items we are helping others. So we win–win all round really!

Helpful tip: If you decide to declutter the whole of your home, this may seem a huge task and momentum can quickly be lost, leading to the project lapsing altogether. To counteract this, decide to declutter one cupboard or an area in one room at a time so that a sense of achievement can be felt, providing the emotional launch-pad each time for the next cupboard or area. Perhaps we should set a realistic time-frame so that by the time of the autumn equinox the whole of the home will have undergone a detoxing and renewal.

23rd March – Mindfulness

When waking today, try setting the intention of practising mindfulness throughout the day. There are many books and much Internet information on mindfulness and, if just starting out, perhaps these few pointers can help:

◈ On waking, pay attention to how your body feels physically; feel the sheets, feel the duvet and consider how your body feels where it touches these areas as well as how it feels where it lies on the mattress.

◈ When rising from the bed, pay attention to which muscles are affected as you do so. Think about what is happening with the muscles in your calves and thighs. When walking down the stairs, consider the actions your muscles are making and try to visualise them moving in co-ordination.

◈ Let's move to the mundane task of washing up after breakfast and feeling the soapy water against your skin. Focus upon the act of washing the cups and plates and notice how they are being washed: are your hands washing in a clockwise direction or anti-clockwise or even both directions? Notice the crockery's ensuing cleanliness and its additional sparkle when you're drying.

◈ At your main meal, pay attention to the food being eaten. Focus upon the taste, its texture in your mouth and how it moves while being slowly chewed. Notice which movements your lips, mouth and tongue make as the food is being chewed. Perhaps you could count how many times each mouthful of food is chewed.

This is a very basic understanding of focusing upon everyday routines that we tend to take for granted. Probably at these times, especially in the morning, most of us are on 'remote control' and thinking of the many things to be achieved during the day while we perform these tasks, so we arrive at 'monkey brain' mode very quickly! Mindfulness of what is happening in the present moment helps us to find stillness and tranquility during our sometimes frenetic lives.

A five-minute yoga routine known as 'prayers to the Earth' is an example of meditative mindfulness, in which our bodies make certain movements and breathing occurs at relevant times to further enable muscle movements. Once the movement routine has been learned, it is possible to enhance the routine practice by visualising colours and sensing aromas. This routine at the start of a workday can help to settle and centre us in preparation for a busy day ahead, by being mindful of the moment with our focus on our movements and breathing, on colour and aroma. This consequently helps us to feel calmer too because at this time we are not thinking of the many tasks facing us.

> "If you are depressed, you are living in the past.
> If you are anxious, you are living in the future.
> If you are at peace, you are living in the present."
>
> –Lao Tsu

So let's try living in the present a little more and be at peace! Research mindfulness today, as its many benefits and avenues of practice may be just what is needed. There are even smartphone apps that can help.

Helpful tip: Also research the 'prayers to the Earth' routine and perhaps adopt it as a regular morning practice.

25th March – The Archangel Ariel

Archangel Ariel is linked with the astrological sign of Aries and is associated with nature, including marine life, animals, devas, fairies and the environment as a whole. He is often petitioned to draw near and assist an animal in need.

Today, we could set a little time aside to pray for Archangel Ariel to help all animals suffering in the world. It can be worded in whichever way we like; there are many examples in books and magazines for those who prefer to follow a structured format. However, a simple, heartfelt and focused request for angelic intervention in their care will be perfectly acceptable.

Helpful tip: To make our intention more meaningful, a prayer whilst walking in the countryside or along the seashore would be appropriate and our attention to the surrounding nature may encourage our prose!

27th March – A Candle for Love and Healing

From today, let us consider a regular practice of lighting candles and each time requesting a blessing of love, light and healing to be sent out into the world; for example, "May the light from this candle send love and healing into my home and on out in the world." Perhaps during times of crisis in the world at large, such as during a time of famine in Africa or when there are earthquakes and floods, we could request specific aid to be sent.

This is an easy practice to adopt and, with many of us sending our heartfelt loving and healing thoughts out to the world, it is an energy that is needed and may just help to make a difference. Each time a candle is lit, we can all create a wonderful ripple effect to bring about change. Wherever your wishes for love and healing are sent, I hope that the love, light and healing from my candles surrounds you too!

Helpful tip: Any colour of candle can be used. However, if you'd like to focus particularly upon nature, animals and wildlife for healing, then a brown-coloured candle would resonate with these energies.

29th March – Ruby, the Aries Birthstone

One of the crystals for Aries is ruby and, whilst the gem quality crystal is expensive, a tumble stone ruby is quite reasonably priced. Ruby is associated with the base or root chakra and helps with revitalising, energising and activation.

Ruby's vibrational energies also help with being optimistic, gaining confidence and finding our inner courage, and thus can further enhance our energetic vibrations in attracting and manifesting opportunities. Therefore, ruby is a good stone to work with this year in helping to accomplish many of the suggestions in this book.

Helpful tip: Perhaps placing a ruby tumble stone in a pocket, to hold occasionally as a reminder of its energies when undertaking new or challenging projects, may be a good idea.

31st March – Starting a Spiritual Journal

If we do not record the events of our life's journey, like a dream they will fade away and become forgotten. Keeping a daily diary can become too onerous though and, instead of being a friend, can eventually be looked on as a chore and be purposely avoided. However, maintaining a journal of events large or small that really stand out as meaningful on our journey can bring us much satisfaction.

It does not matter how insignificant in the great scheme of things we feel an event is, we should consider recording it because although it may have been a small step for us, our overall life journey is made up of many steps, some big and many small. Generally, our spiritual journeys slowly amble along with an occasional acceleration of growth and then a plateau that allows us to relax, practise and consolidate what we have learned before continuing.

Journals can be written in a simple exercise book or a beautiful leather-bound volume; they can even be an artistic scrapbook with affixed items such as photographs linked to a handwritten entry. A journal enables us to record our progress as well as provide a boost for us at times when perhaps we feel as though we have slowed down and our learning has stagnated. Occasionally reading through our previous entries can reboot our motivation and help us to see the wider picture of who we were, where we were at the time, our achievements along the way and thus our future potential.

April

Spring is truly upon us in April. Bluebells and forget-me-not flowers join the greenery of our country hedgerows along with bright buttercups and three-cornered leeks. Rejoice in the Earth's renewal and engage with her beauty.

1ˢᵗ April – April Fools' Day

Today, let's just 'lighten up' as the phrase goes! Have fun, fool around and enjoy ourselves, whether with family, friends, children or on social media. Let's spread the joy of having fun with others. If we play board games we'll change the rules to silly ones, or we'll return to our childhood and play Snap with cards, making fun forfeits.

Trickster myths, stories and legends of gods and animals abound among indigenous peoples throughout the world, so we could surf the Internet today and read about these tricksters.

Helpful tip: If you remember the Roadrunner cartoons with the coyote from the 1970s, the coyote was a trickster with the Native American Sioux people so you could perhaps start with him. Another famous trickster was the Norse god, Loki.

3ʳᵈ April – Sacrifice

Around Easter, the thoughts of Christians focus on the sacrifice that Jesus made for humankind by his death. But many of us can sacrifice our own happiness each day and in effect become unhappy with our whole life. We do this, as the Tarot's Devil card suggests, by placing conditions upon ourselves, creating an imprisoning framework, restricting our thoughts and beliefs and creating self-limiting viewpoints. Out of work hours, we often compensate for our unhappiness by cultivating maladaptive coping mechanisms, habits or activities, which might provide quick fixes and momentary pleasures but overall do nothing to bring us back to the inherent pure joy within us all.

Let us spend a little time in reflection today and consider any part of our lives where the above phrases may resonate. Contemplate whether we can do something about them, whether another option or opportunity can help us better. It's good to think these things over and discuss them with family and friends. Several apparent obstacles can be overcome when the mindset opens to alternatives that enable new relationship patterns to emerge, honouring who we are.

A cautionary word here, though: we should not make rash and drastic changes that consequently make life even more difficult! This is about consciously reflecting and acting appropriately with compassion towards ourselves and others and stepping forward to find new ways.

Helpful tip: The agate crystal is good for self-analysis, and meditation may provide further insights.

5th April – Morning Affirmations

My own morning ritual is to stand in front of a full-length mirror, combing my hair and saying the affirmation, "Mirror, mirror, big and light, my life is wonderfully bright because I live and work in joy, peace, love, excellent health and total abundance of wonderful things, for which I thank the universe and all the divine creators and creations within." It does sounds like a light-hearted fairy story at the beginning; however, why not start the morning with a light heart?

My morning affirmation not only sets my intention for the day to continue in this vein, it reaffirms with my mind and my body that it is so. In reaffirming this energy it travels into the universe, so the universe knows that this is what I wish to continue occurring.

Try positive morning affirmations for yourself and be open to what happens. Affirmations should be in the present tense as if already experiencing their words. Creating affirmations for something to come potentially means that it will always be coming and never arrive!

Helpful tip: One of the great authors of this holistic age is Louise L Hay so, especially if coping with a health condition, research her book *You Can Heal Your Life*. It is a classic read and one that may help with your morning affirmations from a health perspective. She has also written other books of affirmations.

7th April – Plant Spiritual Flowers, Herbs and Fruits

A great many of our plants and flowers have links with spiritual myths, legends, gods and goddesses. If you'd like to consider growing some of them in your garden or windowsill pots, then the following list may contain some that resonate with your spiritual path.

African violet: a symbol of spirituality and protection, sacred to the Greek goddess Aphrodite.

Antirrhinum (snapdragon): protection against curses and deceit.

Chrysanthemum: the Chinese believe that this flower engenders a life of ease and of good luck.

Daffodil: linked with Archangel Gabriel, who is also linked with white lilies.

Geranium: red for protection, white for fertility and pink for love.

Heather: white heather for luck and protection.

Honeysuckle: said to indicate that a witch is in residence!

Jasmine: for aspirations and good intentions. Jasmine's aroma is said to attract angelic energies.

Lily of the Valley: linked with Archangel Haniel, the archangel of joy.

Marigold: linked with the Virgin Mary and also as a flower of good luck.

Primrose: safety and protection, linked with the Fae.

Rose: the widely recognised symbol of love and beauty.

Sunflower: honesty and loyalty, linked with Michael, archangel of the sun.

Wisteria: a symbol of longevity.

Whichever flower is grown, enjoy their beauty and perfume.

Just like flowers, herbs and fruits are also linked with gods, goddesses, spiritual myths and legends and the following list may have one or two to be considered, to grow for culinary or magical work.

Apples: linked with the Greek goddess Aphrodite.

Basil: for prosperity and linked with the Greek goddess Hestia, guardian of the hearth.

Bay: for healing.

Coriander: linked with the Hindu goddess of food and nourishment, Annapurna.

Dill: this is known as Mercury's sacred herb and thus linked with communication as well as justice.

Feverfew and camomile: for health.

Lavender: cleansing and peacefulness, also linked with the Greek goddess Artemis.

Pears: ancient Chinese culture deemed the pear to be a symbol of immortality.

Pennyroyal: for finances.

Red clover: for luck.

Rosemary: for protection.

Strawberry: for love, also linked with the Roman goddess of love, Venus.

Swiss chard: linked with Mars, the energy planet.

Tarragon and marjoram: for confidence.

Thistle and juniper: a home for the fairies.

Thyme: to support healing and work.

So for example, if you experience a general lack of confidence during a difficult time in your life, perhaps growing marjoram and using it regularly in cooking whilst acknowledging its confidence-giving energy may help.

9ᵗʰ April – Help our Bees

Bees are so important to Mother Earth with their pollination of plants. The bees are in danger and require our help in their survival. One way of helping them is to grow plants and even if we're only able to grow some in a small tub outside our homes this will be helpful. Some bees require food all year round and it would be good conservation to create a regular habitat for them.

The following is a list of some plants that will help bees for a large part of the year: rosemary, chives, thyme, lavender, spearmint, hellebore salvia, hebe, ivy, geranium, crocus, Michaelmas daisy, raspberry, apple and pear. Nor should we forget the wildflowers of yarrow, cornflower, plantain, cowslips, meadow buttercup, sorrel and white and red campion. If possible allow the garden hedgerows to grow in wild display and only cut them back at the end of the growing season in order for the bees to have a plentiful supply of wildflower pollen.

Also, we can try making a shelter for solitary bees, putting it in the garden or hanging it on a wall; this would be a good activity to undertake with children as it helps them learn about looking after and caring for nature. An easy option if there's a dead tree stump in the garden is to drill holes in it of various sizes so that solitary bees and other insects can find shelter.

For shamans, Bee energy represent community, rebirth and the goddess. The bees live and work in harmony in their community, working for the benefit of the hive and thus Bee energy reminds us of the same.

11ᵗʰ April – The April Herb Rosemary

Rosemary has many uses and qualities in cooking, magical rituals and herbal remedies. Today, snip a sprig of rosemary and place it in a jar or bottle of mineral or spring water and allow it to sit in the sun for a few hours. When next washing your hair, pour over the rosemary water for the final rinse.

For today's purposes, let's associate the magical use of rosemary as a protective herb and while pouring it over the hair imagine these qualities forming a protective field around the throat, brow and crown chakras. When snipping the rosemary sprig, don't forget to thank the plant for its energies.

Helpful tip: Adding a clear quartz crystal to this rosemary rinse will help to amplify the intention.

13th April – The Songkran Festival

The Songkran Festival in Thailand is their New Year's Day, which they traditionally celebrate by pouring water over themselves to symbolise washing away any bad luck. A good many people return to their home villages in order to celebrate the day with their families as a way of respecting and honouring them.

Festivals of this kind can remind us of strong family bonds, providing a source of familial support and learning. Let's join in Thailand's New Year celebrations today by visiting our own families, sharing a tea party with them and enjoying the time spent in conversation. If successful it may become a regular event in our calendar and used as an opportunity of familial support for the younger generation.

If visiting the family is not possible due to distance or other reasons, then we could perhaps consider joining a local volunteer group that visits people in hospitals and nursing homes, and try lending our support to those in need who may also be lonely. Or we can take this opportunity to befriend an elderly neighbour who has few visitors, spreading a little kindness.

15th April – Passover

Passover is the week-long period of time when Jews celebrate their freedom from historical slavery by the Egyptians, led by Moses. Sadly, slavery continues to this day in many countries around the world.

Let's all light a candle today and when doing so say a prayer for all those in slavery, for them to find their freedom; we could include a wish that the perpetrators and users of this dreadful trade become enlightened to the suffering stemming from their deeds. Let's pray that governments and other relevant authorities become more proactive in ceasing these actions against our kindred spirits. When doing so, we can call upon Archangel Gabriel to help with composing our prayers and then ask Archangel Sandalphon speedily to carry them to God. If our prayers have been written, then we could perhaps consider burning them afterwards, allowing the element of air to carry our words to the universe.

Helpful tip: You may like to research Antislavery International via their website *www.antislavery.org* for further information.

17th April – Blessing Food and Water

All over the world, people bless their nourishment in their own ways such as by a prayer of grateful thanks while sitting around the table about to eat a meal. Wiccans bless the wine and food before passing them around the ceremonial circle. If not already blessing your food and water, try this practice from today.

There are no rules for carrying this out. If you're unsure of what to say in requesting a blessing for food or water, and not wanting to align with any particular deity, then perhaps you could say, "May the universal energies bless this food with its love." If you wish to try this for your pet cat or dog as a starting point, try, "May this be wonderful food for my wonderful pet." A very simple blessing but meaningful.

If blessing food is already a current practice for you, then consider extending it to blessing the food preparation itself. When baking a cake, bless the ingredients before placing it in the oven. When cooking a meal, bless the pans of food in their preparation stages. It only takes a couple of seconds but may make such a difference.

19th April – Archangel Chamuel

The colour associated with Archangel Chamuel is pink and one of the wonderful essences and qualities that this archangel imparts is love, pure unconditional love for ourselves and others.

Archangel Chamuel also helps us to find lost items so try calling upon her for inspiration in knowing where to look for something that has been misplaced. What may occur a little after our request is that an idea simply pops into the mind of a particular room or area in our home or car; this is perhaps where the lost item may be found, or lead us on the route to where we last placed the item.

However, for today let us focus in meditation upon her unconditional love and request her to instil this within our psyche. Many self-help gurus advise those searching for love that they should love themselves first and then this loving vibration will naturally attract love into their lives.

When prepared, we imagine ourselves in a wonderful pink bubble and request Archangel Chamuel to help us love ourselves unconditionally. We ask her to help us acknowledge any areas of personal discomfort we feel about our thoughts and actions in the past; after all, we are human and we all make wrong choices and decisions. Then we request her help in sending a shower of pink to each situation in turn, to heal it with unconditional love for both ourselves and any others involved. We continue with this until it is almost time to finish the meditation, when the final shower of pink is for ourselves. Then we thank Archangel Chamuel for her healing love and set the intention to incorporate this love into our daily lives.

Helpful tip: Hold a rose quartz crystal whilst doing this meditation or, better still, try sitting or lying within a rose quartz grid.

21ˢᵗ April – A Walk in the Countryside

A walk in the countryside today will enable us to experience the joy of the lush hedgerows with plant life beginning to bloom. Flowers will be peeping through everywhere, with blossom on the blackthorn and the sycamore leaves beginning to fan open. Celandines, bluebells, three-cornered leeks and pink campion should promise a colourful display and it is good to see the countryside waking up.

Take a walk in the countryside today or, if you're unable to, visit a local park or gardens and look at the wonderful display that nature provides us with. Feel uplifted and blessed to be in nature and be grateful for its presence in our lives.

23ʳᵈ April – St George's Day

In England, this is St George's Day. He is usually depicted as a knight on horseback, slaying a dragon.

A few years ago I went quite deep into a meditation and there I travelled through space and landed on a planet full of dragons that came to meet me! They were of all colours and sizes. None of them were dangerous and they all greeted me as a long-lost friend. In my meditation, I asked them why they were all on this particular planet and they responded that they had to escape from Earth as otherwise they would have become extinct, being slain through ignorance and fear.

Some maps from the early medieval times show the country of Wales with the phrase 'Here be dragons', indicating a fearful place to be if not Welsh. Today, let's think about our wildlife under threat and therefore in a fearful place. All over the world are habitats where animals indigenous to that area are being hunted and killed to extinction due to ignorance, fear or greed. So let's say a prayer for their wellbeing and do whatever is possible to help these animals.

Helpful tip: Lighting a brown candle and placing aragonite alongside it lends energies sympathetic for wildlife.

25ᵗʰ April – Norse Nine Nights

This period of time recognises the nine nights during which the Norse god Odin hung from the world tree, the Yggdrasil, in order to gain knowledge of the runes. The Hanged Man in the Tarot is linked with this ordeal of Odin's.

When we can understand that sometimes we need a slower pace in life and that occasionally it is better just to wait a while, hang around a little and go along with the flow, it is surprising what can be gleaned from such a period of time. Odin committed himself to nine nights to learn what he thought was important and hanging from a tree enforced the quiet period for him, though I don't recommend the same practice…

Stress is a major factor in many illnesses and indeed is the cause of many, so let us think of the Hanged Man and remember occasionally to take time out and enjoy a slower pace in life, relieving our stresses. We should allow ourselves to find an improved rhythm in life, as we can become lost when continually sustaining the expectations of ourselves and others in an all-consuming existence. During a dormant period of time, our overall health and concentration will improve as our focus is not upon a myriad of tasks, thoughts and actions to be achieved. So go on, hang around for a few days and enjoy the pleasure of it all.

Helpful tip: If you own a Tarot deck, pull this card today and allow its imagery to act as a reminder to consider a slower pace for a while.

27th April – The Seaside at Home

Beaches are wonderful places with their little pebbles in pretty colours or patterns, attracting many of us to pick them up. Seashells are linked with Doris, known as the Sea Goddess, and other sea deities. Mother Mary, the Virgin Mary of the Christian faith, is also called Stella Maris of the Sea and offers protection to fisherman. Let's plan today that when next visiting the seaside we'll collect some pebbles and shells and scatter them around our homes, to invite the wonderful sea energy and sea deities to surround them and bring emotional balance.

Also today, we could carry out some research into seashells; for example, which ones are linked with certain charm work, which ones are linked with sacred geometry and which shells are used in spa treatments?

29th April – The £2 Charm

If you wish to manifest some money for a specific reason, such as paying a bill or purchasing an item for a special occasion, prepare the following money charm to start at the next new moon.

Place twenty-two £2 coins in the shape of a pound sign (or the equivalent in other currencies) and then place three haematite crystals in a triangular shape to encompass it, with two of the crystals at the bottom and one at the top. Haematite is magnetising and will help to attract a flow of money your way. Place this display in your wealth corner (if following Feng Shui), or near your front entrance or perhaps near to where your business accounting is conducted.

Then send your request out to the universe for enough money to come your way to pay for the specific purpose and visualise yourself gratefully paying your bill or purchasing your item with ease and a smile on your face. Light a green candle if preferred to make it more meaningful, adding the boosting energy of fire into the mix. Anointing the coins and haematite crystals with basil essential oil, as basil is linked with finances, could also be considered. Leave this charm in place while the moon is waxing and immediately after the full moon, for abundance and fruition, then remove the coins and crystals and allow the universe to do its work.

In numerology, twenty-two is known as one of the 'master numbers' and is linked with prosperity. However, twenty-two is also linked with altruistically helping others, so when the money arrives be sure to say 'thank you' to the universe and, if there is any money left over after the specific purpose has been fulfilled, then consider sharing some of it as a physical expression of your gratitude.

May

Mother Earth is fertile and now exhibits this in glorious colour and growth. The light evenings help us to express our own fertility in terms of getting out and about and being active and utilising the growing energy from Father Sun. The fire festival of Beltane occurs in May, when Herne of the Greenwood heralds union, vitality and abundant growth at the start of summer. The amusing antics of cats can be seen now that catmint is starting to flower in our gardens, so let them be a reminder for us to be light-hearted and wallow in the lushness of our countryside.

1ˢᵗ May – Beltane Giving Stones

In preparation for the fire festival of Beltane, which celebrates the luxuriant growth of nature and the sun's growing energy nourishing the earth, collect some round, flat stones and take them home for painting. On the flattest side paint, in green, the outline of a spoked wheel so that eight triangles are formed within the wheel. These represent the eight festivals, or Sabbats, to celebrate Samhain, Yule, Imbolc, Ostara, Beltane, Litha, Lammas and Mabon.

To represent Beltane, paint little flowers in bright colours to reflect the fervent growth of nature in all its colourful beauty. Give these to friends and family as token gifts and place one or two in your own garden as a reminder to be grateful and gracious to our planet for her beauty and bounty.

3rd May – Laughing our Socks Off

World Laughter Day takes places on the first Sunday in May each year. Good laughter is such a joy for those laughing and for others to see, so today let's have a laugh. Let's do something or watch something that will cause our core muscles to ache from laughing so much: watch a funny film, play a fun game with the family or friends, watch an old slapstick comedy show.

We could think back to a time when a hilarious scenario occurred in our life, which can produce a good belly laugh once again. Laughter is a vibrant energy, able to lift our spirits. It is said that angels rejoice when we laugh, so from this day of laughter let us reflect upon how much – or how little – laughter plays a part in our daily life and set the intention to laugh more often. Let us be open to the joys of life and be prepared to see and experience humour and light-heartedness, taking joy in observing the laughter of others and joining in as it can be so infectious. Let's have fun today and every day!

5th May – Make a Flower Essence Spray

Flowers are beautiful. When we look closely at the wild hedgerow flowers of cow parsley we notice how their tiny petals mingle to create one large, exquisite flower head. Just like the blackthorn and hawthorn blossom, so daintily pretty. However, also consider the wonderful aroma of plants such as gorse with its evocative reminders of freshly poured pina colada cocktails in the West Indies.

Flower essences are easy to make and it is not necessary to observe any rigid recipes in choosing which flowers to use (although we should certainly stay away from any poisonous plants!). A room spray of roses as a reminder of summer days would be good or perhaps a spray for the bedroom made from peony flowers would be appropriate, as the Chinese consider peonies a love flower. Crab apple is a common blossom to see in the countryside around this time too and according to the Bach Flower Remedies it is linked with helping to find a different perspective of a situation. The beautiful ornamental cherry blossom trees in our parks are a wonderful sight in the spring and an essence of these may be chosen as reminder of beauty in all things.

Making a flower essence is an activity that can be undertaken on a walk with friends or with children. It would be a good idea to take along a book for identification of plants, such as Jo Dunbar's *The Spirit of the Hedgerow*, which also describes the medicinal properties and folklore of plants.

When making a flower essence, try not to touch the flower. Shake the stems first to release any insects and then snip the flower head so that it falls directly into a sterilised jar or into a paper bag for collecting purposes. The best time to collect flowers is mid-morning after the dew has dried and the sun is rising high in the sky and therefore the flowers are full of energy. We should not forget to ask the plant before picking its flowers and afterwards to thank it for its energy.

Using mineral or spring water, soak the flowers and leave the jar outside or on a windowsill to be energised by the sun for a day; then decant the liquid into a spray bottle ready for use. These room sprays make lovely gifts for others and can be packaged up nicely, made with thought, time and effort.

A word of caution, though: this essence is for use as a room spray or aura spray only, never to be taken internally.

Helpful tip: Consider the moon cycle in this particular activity as when the moon is waxing or full it is believed there is more energy within the plant and flower, thus aiding the energetic essence.

7th May – The May Crystal, Emerald

An emerald tumble stone can be purchased from many crystal shops relatively inexpensively. With green being the colour of the heart chakra, emerald's qualities of unconditional and compassionate love for others and for ourselves is a wonderful attribute in assisting our life's journey.

When we operate from an open heart, it helps us to connect with divine grace and so we are open to receiving and being grateful for our lives and enjoying ourselves in the process. Emerald assists us in this respect so we have a double-whammy of open-heartedness working for us. Emerald is also known as a wisdom stone and perhaps the wisdom lies in having an open heart.

Let's research emerald today and if possible buy one to place on the heart area when meditating.

Helpful tip: When a specific matter is of concern, place emerald on the heart centre and be still, as emerald's qualities help us to view the matter from a compassionate, loving perspective.

9th May – Numerology

Numerology is fun, interesting and sometimes downright amazing. From one's date of birth and name it is possible to discover all sorts of characteristics such as personality, life path, destiny, best career, health warnings, desires, compatibility in love, maturity and soul numbers. It is also possible to work out the 'personality' of the home using the number or the house name.

There is a good deal of information about numerology on the Internet and in books and it is easily researched to learn more about.

There are times when it feels natural for us to turn to numerology for further insight in making choices and one example of this is when marriages break down and the wife wonders whether to remain with her married name or revert to her maiden name. Looking up numerology and the energies of the number can help in this choice, so that what is chosen resonates with how she wishes to be.

The numbers in numerology are associated with the letters of the alphabet.

1	2	3	4	5	6	7	8	9
A	B	C	D	E	F	G	H	I
J	K	L	M	N	O	P	Q	R
S	T	U	V	W	X	Y	Z	

Adding up the numbers for the letters in a name leads to the number to read up on. So today you might research numerology and decide whether it is helpful in understanding yourself and others near to you.

Helpful tip: As a starting point for understanding the background of numerology, the ancient Greek mathematician Pythagoras could be researched as he believed that each number has a specific meaning.

11ᵗʰ May – A Crystal Elixir

Crystal elixirs can easily be made for ourselves, our families and for our beloved pets. Tasting tap water and then tasting the same water after it has undergone crystal energising can be an impressive experiment. Crystal energies have been acknowledged for thousands of years and there are hundreds of crystal books, many of which provide instructions for making elixirs and a 'mother remedy'. However, the following simple routine takes less than a minute:

1 Fill a glass jug with tap water.

2 Pour a little into a glass and drink it, sense and taste how it feels such as its temperature, any after-taste and how it feels in your throat as it is swallowed.

3 Hold a rose quartz crystal approximately two inches above the jug of water.

4 Swing a crystal pendulum over the rose quartz crystal and say an affirmation such as, "May the energies of love, compassion and healing of this rose quartz crystal transfer into the water below."

5 When the pendulum has finally stopped swinging or circling, assume the energy transfer is complete.

6 Pour a little of the water into a glass and taste it, checking the difference.

Once this is tried, thoughts such as, 'It tastes like water should taste', or 'It seems cooler' or 'There's no chemical taste' are common. Sometimes, there is a different quality in the water that can be difficult to define precisely, but many quite happily drink their crystal elixir regularly.

Helpful tip: There are hundreds of crystals to use in making elixirs and this indirect method is a good, quick and easy solution. But note that some crystals, such as malachite, whilst having energies required for a particular health reason, are toxic and should avoid contact with the drinking water.

13th May – Hawthorn Month (13th May – 9th June)

The Triple Goddess is associated with the hawthorn because of the white flowers in late spring being the maiden, the red berries of autumn being the mother and the evident bare thorns of winter linked with the crone.

May is a fertile time for the Earth and all her creatures; it's a time for lovers and the hawthorn blossom is linked with love. But if we are seeking love, we should love ourselves first. So let's spend time embracing love and compassion for ourselves today and place some hawthorn blossom around a rose quartz crystal. Then, after grounding and protecting ourselves, we meditate on the heart chakra receiving the loving energies of the crystal. If we are already in a relationship and indeed have a family, we can imagine spreading the love and compassion to our family members and on into our home environment.

Helpful tip: Be mindful of the old superstition of not bringing hawthorn blossom into the home! Perhaps, then, we should conduct this activity in the garden or a quiet spot in the countryside or a park.

15th May – A Travel Charm

Travel charms have existed for hundreds of years. The Christian faith has St Christopher, the patron saint of travellers, and the Greek god Hermes is also deemed a protector of travellers. Travel charms can be made easily, to hang in our cars or placed in our suitcases when going on holiday. They can consist of crystals and various trinkets.

Simply placing a yellow jasper crystal on the dashboard of the car can be surprisingly comforting. Turquoise is also considered as a travel charm and when linked with a silver-coloured trinket of, say, an angel, it could easily hang from the rear-view mirror. Turquoise is especially protective for horse and rider so this may be very relevant for members of your family who ride. Whichever style is chosen and in whichever way it is required as a protection for travel, have fun and be creative in making your travel charm.

Helpful tip: We could make travel charms for our family and friends, to give as token gifts for their birthdays or at Christmas.

17ᵗʰ May – Annapurna

Annapurna is the Hindu goddess of cooking and food. It is believed that if food is cooked and prepared with the intention to provide spiritual nourishment, by linking it with Source and preparing it with care and compassion, then wisdom, knowledge and enlightenment are the end results. What a wonderful way to prepare food for ourselves, family and friends.

So today, plan or prepare a meal for your family or friends, taking time to bless all the food, think loving and grateful thoughts about it, pray over it and not forgetting to bless the water if rice, pasta or vegetables are boiled. Also, bless the room in which the meal will be consumed, along with the table and condiments.

Later, pay attention to how your family or guests responded whilst dining. Were they happier and more sociable than usual? Was all the food eaten whereas normally there would be leftovers? Try this comparison with the routine preparation of a meal and if you notice changes for the better then perhaps this is a new practice to cultivate.

19ᵗʰ May – Extending the Energy Field

We all have energy fields around our bodies and in the summer evenings let's try extending this to keep the midges away! It is easy to do, involving imagination, visualisation and trust that it is being achieved.

Close your eyes and know that your energy field is around your body, like a sheath approximately 10 cm deep. Give this field a bright white colour. Next, imagine expanding this sheath of energy, growing out further from the body until it is about 30 cm deep. Visualise this expanded energy field keeping away midges, trusting that this will happen. It only takes a few seconds but very much worth the small effort when it is extremely effective in doing its job.

Practise this in preparation for the next time midges are out in the evening!

21ˢᵗ May – Candle Magic

There are many ways to use candle magic, including colour, anointing oils, symbols, ribbons and even monitoring how the flames move. Simply by lighting one with the intention of sending love and healing to a sick person is a magical rite in itself. A child blowing out candles on their birthday cake and making a wish whilst doing so is using candle magic.

Let's all try a simple candle magic session today for all those who are falsely imprisoned and whom Amnesty International is trying to help. Their logo is a candle encircled by barbed wire. The use of colour in candles is relevant too and in this instance we shall use white for its intention of purity.

Sit at a table where there is enough room to light the candle in safety and be able to write in comfort. Light the candle and when doing so say something along the lines of, "May the light from this candle send love and healing to all those who are falsely imprisoned." We could think of Shakespeare's words from *The Merchant of Venice*, "How far that little candle throws his beams! So shines a good deed in a weary world."

Focus on the candle flame for a short while, relaxing a little. Now focus on the intention of sending to all those who are suffering and write on a piece of paper what your wishes are for them. Visualise the light of the candle flame as the energy of your wishes and your mental will being released to do its work. When finished, stay in stillness for a while and say a prayer for all those falsely imprisoned. Later, carefully and safely burn the paper with your wishes in the flame of the candle and snuff out the flame.

Helpful tip: Requests can be made for the element of air to carry the smoke speedily from your burned list to the universe for action, or for Archangel Sandalphon to carry your prayer to God.

23rd May – Archangel Zadkiel

Archangel Zadkiel is recognised as the bearer of the Violet Flame of Transformation and practitioners of some forms of Reiki healing call upon this archangel to invoke the Flame with a specific symbol. Transformation can bring about a healing process as the change from one stage or phase to another encourages forgiveness, reconciliation, positivity, compassion, comfort, joy, mercy and benevolence.

For today's meditation, we shall use the colour violet as an aura in which to sit. When comfortable, imagine standing under the shower in your bathroom but, instead of clear water spraying over your body, the water is violet. Visualise your body with violet droplets and rivulets, starting at the head with your hair being bathed in the violet flow of the water, down across your shoulders and arms, back and chest, abdomen, legs and feet. Ask Archangel Zadkiel to allow the violet water to wash away any negativity.

Then visualise the violet colour permeating your internal body, soothing its way through your blood and organs, muscles and skeleton. Finally, visualise the violet colour flowing through your auric fields to help them be open to positivity, joy and compassion. Stay under the violet water shower for a while and, when finished, thank Archangel Zadkiel and request his further help in your everyday interactions with others so that transformation continues. After all, kind words from us can transform someone else's day.

Helpful tip: Hold a piece of amethyst crystal to help with visualising the Violet Flame.

25th May – The Celtic Animal Sign, Seahorse (13th May – 9th June)

Seahorses create an 'Aaah' response in people as they are one of the amazingly cute creatures of the sea. The Celtic animal sign of Seahorse assigns versatility to those born at this time as well as their being lovable and clever.

Being versatile helps us in being able to cope more easily when needing to go from one task to another, from one subject to another or one occupation to another. Becoming caught up with concrete or black-and-white thinking can create unease in our mindset and affect how we conduct our daily routine life, potentially causing us to ruminate too much on unnecessary issues.

Therefore, let's use the energy of Seahorse and try becoming more versatile in our thoughts and actions, allowing opportunities and serendipity to enter and play their part in our lives. If some chance happening feels right, go with the flow.

27th May – The Norse Goddess Frigg

The Norse goddess Frigg, also known as Frigga, is a goddess of love and marriage. The Old Norse name means 'beloved'. Frigg was the wife of Odin and deemed to be the patron of midwives, seen as a protector of women when in labour. Some mothers will light a large white candle in deference to Frigg for her benevolence for when their own daughters commence labour, lighting the candle when labour starts and snuffing it out when their grandchild is born.

Today, say a heartfelt prayer for midwives all over the world for they help to bring about the miracle of birth.

Helpful tip: Archangel Gabriel is associated with childbirth too so consider calling upon him when preparing your prayer as he also aids communication.

29th May – Psychometry

Psychometry is a common activity for people to practise in psychic development groups; items such as jewellery or watches are chosen by others to hold and sit with peacefully, in order to pick up mentally any residual energies emanating from the article. This can be carried out whether the owner is alive or has passed over. Some people sense various emotions or sensations within their bodies, and some readers will also adopt a mannerism of the person the article belonged to, such as running a hand through their hair when this is a habit they do not usually have.

Healers will often sense health issues while others can even pick up names, dates, colours and locations. When sensing health issues, these are mostly felt within the body but without any pain or distress. An example could be that of a watch once worn by a person who suffered a heart attack being used as the article to be 'read'; the person holding it may feel a little light-headed, as if their pulse is racing even though physically this is not happening to them, or perhaps feel as though their breathing is restricted.

Try this with your friends today and, no matter how small or insignificant the sensation, feeling or thought is, do mention it as it may have a huge relevance for the person the item belongs to. Psychometry is a good example of a simple exercise in recognising our sixth sense working and enabling us to become sensitive to subtle changes within and around our bodies. With ongoing guidance and practice our sixth sense can grow.

31st May – Tree Energy

Trees offer life to hundreds of other species, especially insects, and provide a home for our wildlife as well as giving their own lives when deforested to provide wood for our homes and other uses.

Trees offer us and the Earth a great service. When we think of trees being of service, our thoughts often naturally flow to the trees of the great Amazon forest, the lungs of the planet, but we shouldn't neglect the trees on our doorstep. Consider for example the lime trees popularly planted in our towns and cities, soaking up pollution. The yellow flowers of the lime tree are greatly favoured by bees.

Today, find a moment to sit with a tree. Be in its shade and peacefulness and try sensing its energy and how that affects your body. Thank the tree for its service to our world and appreciate its beauty. Afterwards, offer your thanks by perhaps pouring on the roots a little water from a holy well or giving the tree a hug and sending your love to it. Go on, be a tree hugger!

Helpful tip: Record any thoughts or feelings from sitting with the tree in your spiritual journal for later reflection.

June

This month, Father Sun is at his zenith and providing much life force energy, generally noticed as greater activity of the population. June weddings, holidays and many outdoor activities take place. June really does burst out all over with red valerian prolific in our towns, the beautiful Chinese peony, a love flower, blossoming in our gardens and petunias adorning window boxes and hanging baskets, not forgetting the dramatic foxglove in our hedgerows. Enjoy this active month, using the sun's energy to help energise our plans for Litha, the summer solstice, which is celebrated this month. It is a time of beauty, fulfilment and happiness with our radiant sun. The Triple Goddess is also changing from maiden to mother.

1st June – Vision Planning Boards

Vision planning boards are also known as intention boards, energy boards or vibrational boards in order to reflect the energetic vibrations of what we hope to achieve or attract. These boards are A3 or larger pieces of card or hardboard on which, usually, pictures representing our desires are pasted; they help us to focus on our plans, goals and aspirations whether in the short, medium or long term.

However, let's try creating a vision planning board different from the norm today, in that the layout of the board follows the 'pa kua' from Feng Shui as this helps us further in focusing on the different areas of life.

As well as pasting to a large board pictures cut from magazines, try adding appropriate affirmations and mantras. Additional images could be rune symbols, Tarot cards, playing cards and dominoes as certain of these reflect the energy we want to incorporate into our lives. A very enjoyable option is the use of crystal tumble stones as their vibrational energies provide added empowerments.

The vision board can be seen each day as a pleasant reminder for our intended journeys and plans, helping with our focus and also reminding us of being grateful. We should also use the sun's energy at this time as it helps to re-empower any resolutions and intentions that may have lapsed since the New Year.

Have fun creating your board with family or friends, or just by yourself as your contemplative me-time. So many of us have busy family and working lives and do not generally afford ourselves the luxury of a few hours spent in focused contemplation of our goals using artistic means. This could therefore turn out to be a day of pampering our desires.

The pa kua board layout is below, showing the areas of focus for your pictures and embellishments.

Fortunate blessings, wealth and prosperity, good fortune.	Reputation, recognition, fame.	Marital prospects, marital happiness, loving relationships.
Health, family dynamics, ancestors, elders and children.	Spiritual health and wellbeing, life force, chi.	Creativity, luck with projects, luck for our children.
Knowledge and wisdom, study and contemplation, self-cultivation.	Career and work, the general journey of life.	Travel, friends and mentors, helpful people.

Helpful tip: A local framing shop may sell spare mount board, which provides stability if we want to lean our vision board against a wall.

3ʳᵈ June – Strawberries

Strawberries are linked with the ancient Roman goddess Venus, who was considered to be the embodiment of love, and have been called the fruits of Venus. Today, eat some strawberries and simply visualise love enveloping your home and all living in it.

A very enjoyable way to eat strawberries is to dip them whole with their hulks still intact into melted chocolate and place them on a tray to eat later. We could elicit the help of children or other family members in preparing this delightful treat and imagine being encompassed in love whilst all take part. Strawberries are packed with vitamin C and anti-oxidants that fight the free radicals in our bodies. If using dark chocolate with a high rate of cocoa (above 75%) this is also beneficial to health.

5ᵗʰ June – A Dream Diary

We all dream but some of us may sleep very well and hardly ever wake up from a dream and therefore have very few to remember or to make sense of. Some of our dreams allow our subconscious mind to work through queries and difficulties in our lives while we sleep, and can thus provide some insights for our conscious daily life. Therefore, a dream diary can provide much guidance.

It is worth keeping a dream diary by the bedside so that when waking in the early hours it is easy to reach for and write in. To avoid turning on a light and finding the pen, some people simply use the voice recorder of their phone and write the account up next day. It is worth making the effort to record dreams because returning to sleep allows dreams to fade from memory.

At first any dream recording may look like meaningless nonsense but persevering with recording dreams can prove very beneficial; understanding may come gradually, maybe not all at once in one dream but in a series of dreams with each of them playing a part in the whole.

Some crystals can help us with this such as howlite, which enables us to see quite vividly with good recall. By the way, howlite is also considered an aid for insomnia. Labradorite is said to help us tune in to the emotional meaning of our dreams.

For information on dreaming and what can be achieved from them, Anne Jirsch provides an easily understood chapter about the topic in her book entitled *Instant Intuition*, which makes for informative reading. There are many other books giving dream interpretations, while Davina MacKail's *The Dream Whisperer* is a classic on how to use dreams in positive ways, and *Spirit Revelations* by Nigel Peace gives more than one hundred examples of proven prophetic dreams.

Helpful tip: Starting a dream diary at the back of your spiritual journal may be useful, and numbering the pages will also help with cross-referencing dreams of a particular date with events in your life. Also, see the entry for the 15th of July.

7th June – People Watching

Many of us enjoy people watching and for some it is a form of meditative mindfulness, being able peacefully to observe the interactions of others with a non-committal perspective. It is as if two different worlds exist alongside each other and whilst one part of the mind observes all the activities, some of which can be fraught, the other part of the mind is able to focus upon calmness, remaining detached from any angst.

This can really help in workplace situations in terms of being able to acknowledge that many scenarios are occurring but the focus is on the work to be achieved; the observer is able not to become embroiled in the emotions and actions of others unnecessarily. It can also help in meditative practice, in that passing noises from outside can be acknowledged but our thoughts are not attached to them.

Try this today by perhaps sitting at a café window table and watching the world go by whilst calmly sipping a beverage. Do so with your friends if preferable but try not speaking for a while; afterwards discuss together what was observed and the levels of calmness and detachment achieved whilst doing so. Your friends may have observed something that you have no recollection of at all; perhaps instead you found yourself in a true moment of stillness. Try it regularly and monitor your progress in being able to detach from distractions; this will hopefully strengthen your meditation practices as well as your ability to be calm during everyday crises.

9th June – Donation

There are many ways of donating for the benefit of others, whether it is one's time, money or items. In today's media we are asked every day to make a donation to various causes. They pull at our heart strings and leave us wishing to do as much as we can, although some of us will already have chosen areas of donation such as healthcare or animal welfare.

From today, if we haven't already done so, we could consider regularly donating to help others less fortunate. A simple way to achieve this is by placing an item or two of food in the local food bank collecting box each time a weekly shop is carried out, or donating copper coins to a charity tin whenever we receive change. Setting up regular direct debit payments to a charity from a bank account helps greatly but may not suit everyone; however, the above are examples where just a small effort can genuinely help others in need.

11th June – Oak Month (10th June – 7th July)

Oak month is a time for action, a time when previous planning earlier in the year according to the natural rhythm and cycle of Mother Earth should have seen some results by now. The sun is at its zenith in this period and providing much life force and solar energy.

Harness the abundant energy of this time by walking in the countryside or woodlands and find an oak tree to sit below with your back resting against the trunk; then ask the oak for strength and endurance during this busy time. Don't forget to thank the oak tree afterwards. When you get home, record in your journal any differences to the tree energy from the 31st of May. Make a note of what your body sensed with the oak tree energy and any subtle differences.

Helpful tip: If beneficial strength was received from the oak tree, try imprinting this feeling of yourself sitting with the oak tree in your memory. When there comes a time that your energies are feeling depleted, sit quietly for ten minutes and visualise yourself back with the oak tree, sensing its strength infusing your own energy fields once again.

13th June – Gerberas

Gerberas are flowers native to the Transvaal in South Africa and are often seen in florists' bouquets. They are recognised by some to have the healing energy of compassion and are associated with the archangels Jeremiel and Raguel.

Buy some gerberas today and put them in a vase, somewhere it is possible to sit in comfort and be able to acknowledge their simple and natural beauty. Spend a few moments contemplating the beauty of nature, such as the natural creations of the Amazon forest, your local bluebell woods, the Cairngorm mountain range, Ayers Rock, Niagara Falls, the Arctic Circle, the Russian steppes and the patterns in the sand of the deserts…

Each time one of these comes to mind, send a blessing and a healing wish that it will continue to be looked after. Perhaps you could write a list of the beauties of nature if you prefer and at the end draw a heart shape, then bury it in the soil as a gift to our planet.

15th June – Being of Service

In John F Kennedy's inaugural speech as President of the USA on 20th January, 1961, he said the famous words, "Ask not what my country can do for me; ask what I can do for my country." Together with this famous quote there is an interesting line that the late Bob Hoskins said in a film, where he portrayed a butler in a big hotel in Manhattan; he said that being in service does not mean being a servant and thus subservient. Consider also the story of Jesus washing and cleansing the feet of others; he did not think he was subservient, he was being of service to them and showing them the way.

Being of service to others is behaving in a kind manner to help a fellow being, whether friend, colleague or stranger. Even a smile offered to a stranger can lighten their day.

A regular chance to try this is when the supermarket checkout assistants are tasked with asking questions of shoppers as part of customer service standards, such as "How are you today?" Unfortunately, some can sound insincere when doing this because it is a routine for them. However, if we engage with them and continue having a normal conversation it is very likely that we can help them to feel more at ease, so a pleasant interaction between us arises. We can consider this pleasant conversation as lightening our day and theirs.

There are many simple ways to be of service to others and, when this action starts with us, the energy of kindness and respect being sent out to the universe can become contagious.

17th June – The Foxglove

In June, foxgloves take over our country hedgerows as a prolific flower and what a beauty it is too. Look closely at an individual trumpet on the tall spike of the foxglove and note the delicate markings inside. No wonder fairies are often painted wearing foxglove flower hats in children's books, and they are very pretty.

There is a superstition that foxgloves brought into the home means bringing a death into the family. There may be some element of natural healing that has brought about this superstition in that the foxglove is a natural source of digitalis, a substance used in heart health medicine; our healing ancestors using its properties in their work perhaps gave rise to this particular superstition.

As the foxglove's properties are linked with the heart, today let's take some time out and consider our heartfelt actions and whether our thoughts, words and deeds come from the heart. Let us allow the foxglove to remind us to enable our heart to intervene rather than our head always taking over. Allowing our heart to intervene can soften the ego's input into our decisions or actions, thus our inner spiritual navigator is able to guide us in making life-affirming and life-enhancing choices for ourselves and others.

19th June – A Cinnamon Charm

We all wish for good luck and prosperity in our lives and in Wicca a spice associated with luck and prosperity is cinnamon. It is a spice most of us have in our kitchen cupboards and if not it is readily available in many shops. For a little bit of light-hearted magic, give the following charm a chance.

Under your entrance doormat, sprinkle cinnamon powder in the outline of something representing good luck such as a four-leaf clover or a horseshoe, and thank the loving universe for the wonderful luck and prosperity already held. When further luck and prosperity arrives, do share some of it with others.

Helpful tip: Some people do this at a new moon, so that as the moon waxes its energies help to build the energy of the cinnamon charm.

21ˢᵗ June – Litha, the Summer Solstice

Every summer solstice, many people meet up with friends at ancient sites and celebrate the sunrise. These events may take place where hundreds attend, such as at Stonehenge, or for some a low-key celebration at a small site well away from others is preferred. It is a time to express our thanks to the world and request assistance for all those in need, including the planet itself.

Today, let's get up early and watch the sunrise on this longest day of the year and count our blessings in life. It is not necessary to visit stone circles or attend ceremonies, just to wake up early and draw back the curtains in preparation for viewing the glowing orange sun rising in the sky and blessing the day ahead. Be thankful to the life-giving sun, for it provides sustenance for us in all manner of ways.

Helpful tip: If visiting ancient stones, be prepared and take a coat and a flask of hot chocolate to keep warm while waiting for the sun to appear. It may be summer but it is still rather chilly at this time of the morning!

23ʳᵈ June – The Ancient Egyptian Sun God Ra

The ancient Egyptians worshipped their Sun God who, they believed, raced across the sky each day in order to create, sustain and nourish life on Earth. Ra was a father-figure god, masculine in energy, who nurtured life on Earth for us all. We often equate nourishment and nurture with feminine and motherly energies these days and can forget about the fathers who are in the background, often working hard to ensure the family is provided for.

Around this date, Father's Day is celebrated in the UK. So as the Sun God Ra is still high in the sky let us turn our thoughts to those fathers who spend time with their children by playing football or cricket, building sandcastles on the beach, and sitting with their children to help with homework, encouraging their learning. Remember those fathers who provide care for their children in all the ways they are able to.

Let us say a hurrah for those who are house-husbands and proud of being so, especially for those who led the way in the early days for they had the courage to do so. Let us recognise that fathers also provide nurture for children and send gratitude for their nurture into the universe, praying that they continue to be a beacon of light to all males learning how to develop the quality of nurture in their own lives.

25th June – The Chariot

In the Tarot, the major arcana card of the Chariot is linked with the astrological sign of Cancer. This is about new directions being pursued.

Today, then, is a time to reflect on our spiritual path, our life journey, to question whether we are moving forward on this path and with our spirit. We need to question whether this is what our higher self wishes to achieve and whether any change in direction is required or an acceleration of growth.

We should try not to be dismissive of what has been learned and experienced so far, for life is one huge learning process and sometimes we cannot immediately tell how valuable lessons have been. Moving along the right road in the right direction and in balance is what we aim for but sometimes we need to decide whether a change is called for. If life feels a little stagnant or stuck, then perhaps we should change direction, even if it's only a small change, in order to re-energise forward movement. Do we have standard thoughts and fixed ways of doing things in our spiritual lives? A small change can totally alter the trajectory of our lives and lead us to a stimulating new destiny.

Helpful tip: If intending to make changes, try not to leave these for too long as the sun is only at a high point for a little while and we can use its wonderful energy to help energise our new directions.

27th June – Archangel Haniel

Archangel Haniel is known as the angel of joy and is associated with the many shades of red. We can find joy in so many areas of our lives: the love we share with our family and friends, the creative hobbies we undertake, achieving our tasks at work and the joy of simply being alive on this wonderful planet.

Today, prepare for meditation and imagine yourself in a bubble that has a shade of red or swirls of many red shades. When ready, visualise yourself surrounded by red admiral butterflies, symbols of transformation, flitting about in joyful fashion with some landing on your body and fanning their wings. Feel the joyful release of any pent-up emotions leaving your body and allow the red admiral butterflies to transform these negative emotions. Stay watching the butterflies for a while and meditate upon the joys in life, because they are there, they just have to be recognised and acknowledged. As your meditation progresses, one joy begets another.

When the meditation is finished, thank Archangel Haniel for her joyful energy and go out for a walk. Keep a lookout for any butterflies, expressing thanks to them too for their joyous beauty.

29th June – Cosmic Ordering

In the New Testament of the Bible, Matthew, 21.22, it is said, "If you believe, you will receive whatever you ask for in prayer." Is this one of the first recorded examples of cosmic ordering? Barbel Mohr, who died in 2010, is probably the most popular author of books on this subject, although there are many well-known people who advocate cosmic ordering.

Searching for the subject on the Internet, a huge array of information arrives at our fingertips. If you have not yet tried cosmic ordering, give it a go today. If you are already cosmic ordering, then perhaps consider expanding your orders.

Some believe that cosmic ordering is linked with the power of positive thought and 'the law of attraction', having positivity and trust in our requests and attracting our desires. So it's best not to request something when in a negative mood, nor to use negative words or phrases with a request. A good example of this is one who says, "I never win a prize when I buy a Lottery ticket so make me win..." Also, it is best not to phrase one's request as something to arrive in the future, because it will then always be in the future and never actually arrive.

Once our request has been made, then it is passed over in trust. This begs the question of who or what are we passing it over to? The universe, family members in spirit, angels, guides? Perhaps it is a combination of all these as they are energies of the universe and the energies of the universe react to our own thoughts, consequently bringing about the law of attraction. Trust in the process is vital because meddling or fretting about it each day can block the flow of the universe in working its magic.

It is also helpful to recognise that when our order has arrived it may not be as clear as hoped for or quite what we expected! Sometimes the universe works in unusual ways. An example of this could be that of requesting the funds to buy a car, but what then appears is the option to buy a works car at a reduced cost that suits our finances perfectly.

And just like wishes, we need to be careful what we ask for because we might just receive it!

One other point to consider is to help ourselves when making an order by creating the right conditions. For example, if our request has been to meet more friends then we should 'put ourselves out there'. The universe would struggle to fulfil this request if we remained at home all the time without communicating with other people. So it would be important to consider attending classes that interest us or other public events, where we can gradually socialise with others and allow this type of opportunity to help the cosmos bring our wishes to fruition.

When ordering, some people prefer detail while others just say what's in their heart. Some use the time of the full moon while others make requests at special personal times. One very important final consideration is that when our cosmic order has arrived, it is important to thank the universe.

Helpful tip: Barbel Mohr herself described a cautionary tale from her own life to consider when making a cosmic order for a new relationship, with a detailed list of the physical characteristics desired. Such a person duly arrived, but proved totally unsuitable as a partner!

July

Warm sunshine, balmy evenings, ripening grain in the countryside and seaside picnics! This is a lovely month for celebrating life.

1ˢᵗ July – Antahkarana

There are two antahkaranas, one masculine and one feminine. They appear in Tibetan, far eastern and Buddhist faiths. The antahkarana is an ancient symbol formed by an equal-armed cross with each arm continued at a right angle. This form was used for the German swastika. However, its original meaning has not wavered for those who respect it: 'svastika' is Sanskrit for wellbeing. There are different ways of looking at an antahkarana: for example, it can look like three sevens or, from another perspective, a three-dimensional cube.

In our lives, it is good to feel balanced with both masculine and feminine energies so an easy way to accomplish this is to place one each of the masculine and feminine antahkaranas under the bed where we lie, to reflect each of the energies beneath us.

You could research these images today on the Internet and print off a copy of each. Whether male or female, we all need a balance of feminine and masculine energies.

3rd July – The Feast of Cerridwen

This day is known as the Feast of Cerridwen, a Welsh goddess of transformation. Cerridwen was said to have 'a cauldron of inspiration' and there is a legend surrounding the contents of her cauldron. It was being stirred by her servant in preparation for her son, but the servant received the cauldron's contents of wisdom instead and not the son as intended.

Today, let's create our own cauldron of inspiration by first simply finding the time and space where we can sit in peace and not be disturbed; switch off the phone, television and radio (although gentle meditative music on a CD may be good in the background). Then make a beverage such as hot chocolate or herbal tea, relax and put the feet up.

Hold the mug of hot chocolate near your lips and look into the liquid, allowing the eyes to relax, almost as if having double vision. Gently allow your mind to sift through and mull over a creative idea or a task that needs to be considered and let the mind wander over the thoughts and potential options available. Socrates said, "Wonder is the gateway to wisdom." Daydream with the possibilities and allow all sorts of inspiration to stir in your thoughts. Then slowly sip the beverage, enjoying this peaceful moment of the day and basking in the opportunity to flirt with the many ideas that arise while doing so.

You may just have a 'eureka moment' of inspiration, suggesting a sounder foundation upon which the task or creative idea can be achieved.

Helpful tip: If other, unconnected thoughts start to intrude, just acknowledge that the mind has strayed a little and gently let them go like a passing cloud, returning to the task in hand without becoming irritated.

5th July – Saraswati

Saraswati is the Hindu feminine deity of knowledge, music, arts, wisdom and learning. She also guides us in self-learning. Today, we might try finding some more time to be in stillness and allow our thoughts to muse gently around these aspects, considering how we could grow further on our life's journey with learning and wisdom. We can petition Saraswati for her assistance by lighting either a yellow candle to reflect intellect and study, or a purple one for wisdom, and have to hand an item that epitomises learning such as a dictionary or reference book.

We should also think of ways to help the children or younger family members with their learning or whether it is possible to volunteer our time and skills with the local youth community for their learning. Life is one long learning process for us all and if we embrace this and accept the flow with all that it brings, opportunities can arise both for ourselves and others.

If we block potential learning by thinking that we are 'old enough and wise enough' already and do not need to learn any more, or we do not wish to learn from those younger, we create a barrier that stops us experiencing so much that life has to offer. Our beliefs are real energies and forming a resistive energy of learning from others, whom we perhaps deem irrelevant to us, does little to honour them or ourselves. We can grow and learn in so many ways at various stages in our lives and from various people and circumstances. Even a child may, for example, innocently voice the most resounding phrase that can sit in our minds as a check-in barometer for us in times of stress when perhaps we are not functioning at our best. This then reminds us that self-knowledge and self-learning arises in many and varied guises.

Helpful tip: A tumble stone of ruby may help here as it sharpens the mind and improves concentration, whilst sugilite also helps with group communication.

7th July – A Time-Out Meditation

When we are working – whatever form that takes – we occasionally reach a point of overwhelm; perhaps this is the moment to down tools and try a 'time-out meditation' to enable us to return to our work and approach it once again from a calmer perspective.

An easy way to achieve this is to sit down, close the eyes and start breathing slowly and regularly for approximately one minute. Then, we visualise a big fluffy, white cloud in the shape of the figure '30'. We imagine slowly breathing in this shape and feeling the air entering our lungs and cleansing the whole body; then we slowly breathe out, visualising dirty brown smoke leaving the lungs and the body. This out-breath should take a little longer than the in-breath.

The next step is to visualise the figure '29' now as a big fluffy, white cloud and breathe this in and so on, following the sequence reducing down to '0'. When we are used to this time-out meditation, our breathing pattern will become slower and it will take longer to breathe in and out, so counting down from a '20' cloud will probably be ample.

The reason for counting down is that it is so easy and normal for us to count up that it requires little mindfulness; however, counting down helps us in being mindful of the next number in the countdown. If we practise this today, we shall soon be ready to call upon it when required.

Helpful tip: If it is awkward in the workplace to find a place to sit in peace, then perhaps a visit to the washroom may be the answer! It's not ideal but there will always be a solution, depending on our work circumstances.

9th July – The Horse Sign (8th July – 4th Aug)

Horse in the Celtic animal calendar suggests that people born during this period are valiant and talented. What are horses if not valiant and talented, among their other great attributes? Just read the famous poem by Ronald Duncan entitled *The Horse* for a wonderful description of this noble species[1].

From today, let's think of the qualities of Horse and try to emulate them in our daily lives. Let us stop denying or dismissing our talents and instead acknowledge, respect and enjoy them, bringing them to the fore in our lives. These talents may be a pathway of bringing fulfilment not only for ourselves but for others too, acting as a beacon for them to make the conscious choice of following their own inner desires.

Let us resolve, too, to be valiant in the face of our adversities and challenges in life, not forgetting to be gentle at the same time; just think of those gentle giants of agriculture and dray stock with their huge power. We can learn from them.

Helpful tip: Equine therapy is gradually growing and becoming recognised as a genuine complementary therapy, especially for the disabled or those with mental health issues. Researching this today may enable us to understand better what these amazing animals can accomplish.

11th July – Blue Light Service Prayers

The flashing blue lights of the police force, the ambulance and fire services, are often seen on our roads dashing to or from an accident or incident. Nor should we forget the coastguard.

---

1   I admit to a little personal bias in respect of Horse as I believe there to be a spiritual horse around me, which a medium has advised is one of my animal guides; a shaman has also told me that Horse is my animal totem as I journey along my life.

From today, we could consider starting a practice of offering our own little prayer for the highest and greatest good of everyone involved in such crises. This is meant for those being saved, rescued or treated and also for the blue light personnel themselves, so that they may remain safe too and make the right choices and decisions in their emergency work.

One day, it could be you or I or a family member or friend who requires a blue light service… consider how grateful we would feel if we knew that total strangers had prayed for us or our loved ones, and that the energy of the prayers had helped? Indeed, Reiki and other healers often do 'send' healing energy or visualise a Reiki symbol on an emergency vehicle as it passes.

13th July – Sleep Hygiene

At this time of the year when humidity and light evenings can disrupt our sleep cycle, it is important for us to try to observe a regular sleeping pattern; eight or so hours sleep each night assists our bodies in maintaining good health. There are many methods recommended, apart from prescribed night-time sedatives, to enable a good sleep and some of them are given here.

◈ Ensure time is spent outside as fresh air and being outdoors helps our body to function appropriately, expending energy and being active, and then when it's time to retire to bed our energies are ready for rest. But don't do any strenuous exercise just before bedtime; if you like to do some stretches, then perhaps a few gentle meditative hatha yoga positions may be suitable.

◈ Eat only a light evening meal, and not too late, so that food does not lie heavily in the stomach at night. A herbal tea such as camomile, perhaps sweetened with honey, about an hour before going to bed has a soporific effect. Hot milk is another option.

◈ If you like a bath before bedtime, make sure it's warm and not hot, and add a little lavender essential oil for its calming and soothing aromatherapy notes. A good idea is to mix three drops of lavender essential oil with two tablespoons of milk before pouring this mixture into the bathwater; this helps the essential oil to merge better with the bathwater.

◈ Reflexology can be incredibly relaxing and it's possible to carry out a form of this ourselves while lying relaxed and flat on the back in bed. First, expand and stretch the soles of the feet by bringing the toes up and stretching them towards the knees. Then one by one bend each toe in turn towards the soles of the feet so that the soles also bend over forming a gentle arch. Continue with this movement very gently, twenty times for each foot. This action massages many of the Reflexology points of the feet, thus aiding peacefulness and a sense of calm.

◈ Some like to count sheep but another form of counting is more effective. Once relaxed and comfortable, pay attention to the breathing and slow it down. Then count down from 100, with each gentle breath in and out being one count. Counting down in this mindful manner is better than counting up because our minds focus on the unusual counting pattern and breathing and are not focused on any stresses. Often, by the time we reach about 70, our counts go awry such as counting breaths as 69, 67, 65, 68… and this is just before falling asleep.

◈ The actual décor of the bedroom plays a part in how peaceful we feel. Stimulating colours such as reds and oranges are not conducive for restful sleep. Instead, consider calming and balancing colours in pastel shades such as light blue and green shades, with a few bright scatter cushions if you want some extra colour. Heavy curtains for the windows may also be a good idea, to ensure that light is shut out. If at all possible, do not place the bed with a window behind the head and especially not within a bay window area, as this creates a stimulating effect.

◈ Electricity near to us can disturb our energy so there should be no televisions or computers in the bedroom and lamps should be switched off at the socket. Swapping a mains alarm clock for a battery operated one is also preferable. If space is at a premium and it's necessary to have a television or computer in the room, then position them away from the bed and if possible behind a screen, to separate daytime activities from sleep time. A peace lily plant or a sodalite crystal placed near electrical equipment can soak up their electromagnetic 'smog', which could otherwise disturb sleep. Finally, if the bed is under the room's centre light perhaps the best shade to use would be an uplighter type so that the electrical energy is deflected.

Sleep tight and don't let the bedbugs bite!

15th July – Dream Colours

Staying with the subject of sleep, placing a fresh bay leaf under the pillow on going to sleep tonight is said to promote prophetic dreams. Or, on the night of the dark of the moon, try a fresh sprig of mint. For those with good dream recall this may enhance the guidance received (see the 5th of June entry). The phrase 'sleep on it' is very pertinent, as many people like to allow their thoughts to be worked on by the subconscious, subsequently waking up with a determined course of action.

Our dreams can be very symbolic and difficult to decipher but noting that a certain colour is prominent in the dream can be very significant. An example is that red being an overriding theme suggests passionate feelings. However, such feelings can range from feeling passionate about our lovers or even being passionately angry towards others. A colour therefore needs to be seen alongside other visions and symbols occurring in a dream. If we later realise that our dream was symbolically linked with a difficult situation being encountered in our life, one that we feel resentful about, then perhaps red denoted anger.

But when anger is held within the body it can bring about disease; so our prophetic dream may be reminding us to find alternative solutions to the situation, preferable to our continuing to seethe with anger.

Suppose we dream about falling from a ladder at a great height while painting and decorating. The symbolism of falling, of the ladder and of the activity of decorating are obviously all important; but what about the colour of the paint? When everything is put together it is possible for us to understand what the dream is telling us to be mindful of in our waking day.

So try utilising the magical properties of bay, or mint on the dark of the moon, to further enhance your dreams tonight and seek to interpret them.

17ᵗʰ July – Collecting Seashells

On this day visit a beach, or plan to visit one, to collect seashells to bring home. Make sure to have fun whilst doing so and find as many varieties as possible, large and small. Thank the Great Mother or the sea goddess Doris for the shells.

If there's time while on the beach, place the shells in a circle and sit inside it to meditate for a while, allowing the sounds of the sea and the gulls and the flow of clouds in the sky to carry away any thoughts or concerns and help you relax. Find your still point and simply be at peace with your body, allowing nature to imprint itself upon your memory so it can be called upon whenever meditating with the seashells at home.

The different shapes of shells have different energies and are used in healing layouts by some practitioners. Our common clams, limpets, cockles and whelks each have a specific energy.

Helpful tip: Daya Sarai Chocron's book *The Healing Power of Seashells* may be helpful if you'd like to research the energies of seashells. It also offers simple suggestions for healing layouts and grids.

19th July – A Wish in the Sand

When visiting the seaside at low tide, we could draw a wish in the sand so that, when the tide comes in, it encompasses our wish and in this way a natural element of Mother Earth has taken the wish out to the universe. If unable to visit today, then we can plan our future wishes in the sand, writing them down ready for when we go.

For example, we could draw a house to represent our home. We give it windows and a door, but leave the door open for the tide symbolically to enter freely, even drawing an imaginary pathway for the flowing tide to follow. In the middle of the house we draw whatever is wished for, such as a £, $ or € sign if we need extra finances, a car if that's what we need, or a smiley face if we wish for everyone at home to remain happy and joyful.

Then we leave the wish behind in the sand and allow the universe to do its part. Try starting this practice from today and make a wish each time there is a visit to the beach or other tidal waterway. When we are leaving, we must not forget to thank the sea goddesses and the element of water for their support.

Helpful tip: If we can rarely visit a beach yet there are several wishes to be considered, draw three of the above images side by side in the sand with a representative symbol in each one. This utilises the magical 'power of three' for our wishes.

21st July – A Higher Self Meditation

Today, try a meditation to connect with your higher self, your intuition or your soul, using a quartz crystal to amplify the meditation. Firstly, ground and protect yourself (see the entry for the 11th of January) and then hold the crystal cupped in your hands, finding your still point.

Imagine yourself in a large and beautiful garden with many smaller sections, each of which is surrounded by shoulder-high hedging. Wander around the large garden… the first hedged section to arrive at is a rose garden where you can see the glorious array of chakra colours of the many roses. Sense their perfumes too, permeating your energy field and allowing you to relax further. Stay a while and walk slowly around this rose garden, enjoying your time.

When you're ready, walk through to another section where there are rows of various herbs and visualise the bees visiting the thyme and lavender especially. Imagine touching the various herbs as you wander around, noticing their aromas as their aromatic energies are wafted around with your hands. Here, you start to feel in tune with nature and the natural cycles of life.

After very slowly walking around the herb garden, you then arrive at another area filled with buddleia bushes of vibrant purple and violet colours. You notice a lot of movement around the buddleia flowers and then realise that this garden is full of butterflies, which are attracted to buddleia. As butterflies represent transformation, stop and sit upon a comfortable wooden seat and think about what these butterflies represent for you on your journey.

After sitting in the sunshine for a while feeling relaxed, visualise a glowing light body appearing next to you on the garden seat. This light body feels familiar. As you pay more attention you notice that there's a white cord from your solar plexus to their solar plexus – this light body is your higher self. Express your gratitude to your higher self for appearing and ask for help in understanding what you need to know or be mindful of at this stage of your journey. After a few minutes, allow your body and your light body to integrate and become one again. When comfortable with this melding, rise from the garden seat feeling renewed and thankful of the learning from your higher self.

As you leave the garden, say goodbye and thanks to the plants and butterflies for their help. Then visualise yourself entering the room you were in when starting the meditation; start to feel your body against the chair, wriggle your toes and fingers, move your feet and stretch your arms before opening your eyes.

Helpful tip: When ready, make sure to write down any new thoughts or images that have come to mind during the meditation, or later during the day, and consider their meaning.

23rd July – The Feast of Sulis

An ancient British-Romano goddess of springs was known as Sulis and this day was celebrated as her feast day. Today, let us send healing thoughts to all springs in the world.

An interesting way to do this is to purchase a floating candle and light it in a bowl of water. When doing so, we might say something along the lines of, "I light this candle to send healing thoughts and energies to all springs, wells and water supplies in the world." We sit in peace for a while and as the candle burns we focus the mind on waters throughout the world, visualising them running clean, clear and pure, and the areas surrounding them being bathed in a white glow of love and purity. We can add a prayer for these waters to run pure and clean for humans, animals and for the environment.

Further, we could consider whether we're able to make a donation to those organisations dedicating themselves to helping developing countries to source clean water supplies.

Helpful tip: A lithium quartz crystal would be ideal to place nearby while conducting the above ritual, as this crystal's benefits include purifying water.

25ᵗʰ July – Tiger's Eye, the Leo Birthstone

Tiger's eye is an easily obtainable crystal that reminds us of our talents and abilities and builds up our feeling of self-worth when it may have been slightly hurt. It can remind us to operate with a sense of harmony and to find balance in our lives. When out of balance, the body's harmonic vibrations can feel a little awry and our emotions become trapped, leaving us feeling a little out of kilter.

With its dual colouring, tiger's eye is linked with the base chakra for grounding and also the solar plexus chakra where we feel our emotions. Thus it can help us to be more grounded whilst working on any emotional turbulence being felt.

So today, research tiger's eye and buy one of these very inexpensive crystals in preparation for when it is required to assist us with letting go of old habits or addictions, to make way for new and positive patterns that will enhance our abilities and self-worth.

27ᵗʰ July – A Change of Perspective

Changing our perspective of a situation can help us greatly along our life's path. It allows us to consider something from a different viewpoint, which can have immense implications for something that might have been holding us back.

In shamanic practices, Eagle energy enables one to take a bird's eye view of something, with a huge vista emerging in which we may notice something not previously taken into account and seeing that which others cannot see, with Eagle's incredible clear sightedness.

Let us try a change of perspective today and think about something problematic to us. It could be our reactions to a certain person, or it could be a fear of something occurring if we follow a certain course of action. It could be a conditioned response we're aware of when something or someone triggers a reaction in us. It could be a fixed view of something that we recognise is detrimental to us or others, so that we feel as though we are treading water...

Let's ask what an eagle would see if they were looking down from high above, observing all the internal and external parts of the scenario in a non-judgemental way. Then let's take a little time to ponder over what we might change in our situation or how we might think about it differently. We may realise that we've had fixed views of an issue that have caused distress for ourselves and those around us, so we should consider changing our perspectives.

But let's not forget to be kind to ourselves today, too, as changing our perspectives brings about changes that enable a reinvention of life for ourselves and others.

29th July – Archangel Raziel

Archangel Raziel is known as 'the keeper of universal mysteries, secrets and the power of the cosmos' so if we're doing manifesting work or cosmic ordering then Archangel Raziel's energy can assist us further. (See the entry for the 29th of June too.)

He is linked with the mystical and sacred awakenings in people on their spiritual journeys, helping with insight and clarity; thus if we want more tangibly to sense and understand divine guidance and interventions, we could call upon Archangel Raziel for his help. We prepare by using the rainbow of colours associated with the archangel: a clear calcite crystal with the rainbow spectrum seen in its fractures may help with visualising a rainbow. This is also a crystal that can encourage us on our spiritual paths, so perhaps we could hold one in the lap.

We start by imagining ourselves in a clear bubble of protection, just like the bubbles that children blow, and we visualise the rainbow colours reflected in the bubble swirling around us. Then we ask Archangel Raziel to help us in trying to understand the universe and our part within it. We now imagine the air within the bubble turning red, permeating every part of our body, cleansing, purifying and healing. Then the bubble turns orange and works in the same way as before, continuing on through the remaining rainbow spectrum of yellow, green, blue, indigo and violet. Finally, we thank Archangel Raziel.

Trying this meditation regularly will hopefully bring new intuitive insights.

31ˢᵗ July – Janus and the Golden Age of Rome

The ancient Roman god Janus was depicted with two faces, looking in opposite directions to represent past and future or start and ending. It is thought that Janus was associated with, and perhaps responsible for, their 'golden age' in terms of trade, wealth and agriculture, which brought stability for them.

Today, let's think about our current agricultural, forestry and other farming industries and say a prayer for those taking care of the land of Mother Earth in these ways. Like Janus, look to the past when crops were grown without being modified and harmful chemicals were not used. Now look to the current and future practices and pray that those responsible consider carefully and clearly their actions in looking after the land, that they may be insightful of their practices and make changes where there is potential harm. We should pray, too, for them to consider the animal, bird and insect species indigenous to their areas and practise safe husbandry for these to thrive.

A prayer is also needed for the governments throughout the world that they engender compassionate attitudes towards the Earth. Huge agrochemical companies hold such power when it comes to lobbying for their products so let's pray that they work more harmoniously and less aggressively in order to aid, honour and respect our wonderful planet.

Helpful tip: Rainforest jasper is a crystal linked with the element of earth, with earth healing and with our connection to nature, so holding a piece of rainforest jasper at this time can enhance our prayers.

August

It's the time to celebrate our cereal harvests with Lammas. We are blessed with the gift of ripening corn in our countryside and an appreciation for the bounty of Mother Earth is in our thoughts. There is bright orange montbretia in our gardens and growing wild in the hedgerows. Aromatic sweet peas are picked by children and placed in simple jam jars on kitchen tables. These are warm, lazy summer days spent with the children during the school holidays. Good memories to capture forever.

1ˢᵗ August – Blessing Cupcakes

Try to wake up early today to bake some cupcakes, not forgetting to bless the ingredients. When spooning the mixture into the individual containers, slip into each one a piece of folded greaseproof paper which has written on it an uplifting phrase such as, "May joy be your companion" or, "May the sun shine upon you forever."

They could be included in a picnic to celebrate Lammas, the first harvest, with family or friends or even at lunchtime with work colleagues. These cupcakes are similar to Chinese fortune cookies but much more meaningful as they have been baked and blessed by your hands. Share food with others on this day and be thankful for the bounty of nature.

Helpful tip: If you've never baked cupcakes before, this is the day to try! They are not hard to make: go online to find recipes.

3rd August – A Prayer for Dangerous Drivers

From today, whenever reckless, aggressive or dangerous driving is seen on our roads please consider praying for the driver behaving in this manner. This is for the driver to become calm, stable and attentive to what they are doing and to be mindful of others so that all around them remain safe.

In this way, instead of us thinking that we need to remain clear of these drivers and leave them to deal with their own outcomes, as if shrugging off any responsibility, we are adopting a proactive approach in requesting help for them. Whether our petition is to God, Source, another protective deity or to guardian angels and spirits, what matters is our acknowledging that real help is needed for them in the interests of the safety of others as well as the driver.

Sometimes we believe that people learn by experience and so the results of dangerous driving bring about a meaningful lesson for the culprits, acting as a catalyst to understand their errors and subsequently helping them to change. This is similar to police forces providing the option of lectures and films for drivers caught speeding. Whilst these may prove beneficial, we should remember that some drivers ignore such advice or may even never be caught out; therefore prayer is very much an active option for us to offer.

5th August – Hazel Month (5th Aug – 2nd Sept)

The time of hazel month is an opportunity for us to connect with our intuition and with nature. On this day, we could locate a hazel tree and make a divining rod from one of its long twigs. Firstly, though, we should thank and bless the tree with an offering of life-giving water if we need to cut the twig; it needs to be in the form of a Y-shape and be approximately 90 cm in length.

We cleanse and dedicate the divining rod by sprinkling it with water from a holy well or passing it through the smoke of an incense stick, whispering to the rod our intentions for its use. We're going to have fun but also informative practice with it as a divining tool.

We hold the divining rod so that the prongs are in each hand with our palms upwards, then pull the prongs apart gently until tension is felt. Be prepared! When the rod indicates that water has been found it can twist hard in the hands and smack against the legs, or for some people the rod can make an upwards motion.

To practise with our divining rod, we first set our intention by telling it that our desire is to locate water, for example, and concentrate on visualising water; then we walk along outside until we come to a pre-placed container of water and note the actions of the divining rod. We continue to practise in several ways, being innovative, until we are comfortable with trying more difficult scenarios where, perhaps, another person has hidden water or an item to be found.

This kind of divining is also known as dowsing or water witching and is a practice used to locate hidden water, buried metals, gemstones and other objects. The instructions here are very basic so please research it in more detail today.

Helpful tip: Metal dowsing rods could also be tried, purchased from many MBS shops; however, some people are even adept at making a dowsing rod from bending a wire coat-hanger!

7th August – Make a Wand

You might try making your own wand today, whether for serious use or just as a fun display. If it's not for your personal spiritual work, you could include children in the wand-making session too and use all sorts of sparkling glitter and ribbons. But carefully consider what the wand is to be used for and then have a go; it may be so much more meaningful than one purchased in a shop.

Wands are used for many purposes such as casting protective circles for ceremonial or charm work, and crystal wands are used in healing work. If you'd like to make your own wand for charm work then certain trees have associations to be considered:

Ash is for healing and is linked with the element of water;

Hazel is for white magic, knowledge, personal growth and healing;

Elder is for purification and love, linked with the goddess Venus;

Oak is all-purpose use but especially for strength, protection and longevity, being linked with Hercules, Zeus, Jupiter, Herne and Cerridwen;

Willow is used for healing and is linked with Artemis, Hecate and Persephone.

Helpful tip: The above is not a comprehensive list and, as different woods reflect different uses for wands, research this on the Internet so that the best wood is chosen for your needs.

9th August – What's Your Glass Like?

This has become a common phrase to ask people, used as a measure to help them understand how they feel life is treating them. Is yours 'half full'? From today, try thinking of your glass being full to overflowing! Know that this is a conscious choice of living, of how we view, feel and experience life.

When trials and tribulations arrive at our doorstep, it is how the situations are dealt with that matters. A defeatist mindset can engender a lack of direction, impoverished images, unsustainable habits and a general loss of resolve. If life were a bowl of cherries and never presented us with challenges, how could we continue to grow and learn? An extremely difficult person, for example, could turn out to be our biggest teacher! Although we may never be bosom pals, we should perhaps be grateful to them for personally stretching our abilities and learning skills in dealing with their demands. Mostly, our instinctive desire is to lead good and enjoyable lives in contentment and peace with others; so being able to maintain this while acknowledging our challenges helps to define our character and create a different reality within our mindset.

The phrase 'This time too shall pass' can really help when dealing with challenges, so that our cup remains overflowing because of the potential personal growth on our life's journey. Changing our mindset to this very positive framework can create the like-attracts-like scenario and positivity in all areas will be attracted to us in turn. Positively manifesting and elevating our thoughts and vibrational energies enables a joyous approach, allowing the universe to flow into our glasses – to full and overflowing.

11ᵗʰ August – Your Own Special Prayer

Do consider the power of this idea even if you do not normally say prayers, as many people do every day. Some prayers are petitions for others and can be just a few sentences in length while of course we often pray for ourselves too. Prayers can feel like comforting friends and are part of many people's daily meditative process. Very often, they are prayers set down for us by our faith or ones that we were taught long ago. Now, why not try creating your own special, personal prayer to say every day, perhaps one that reflects your current life and includes expressing gratitude, which also acts as a life-affirming statement? As life continues, this prayer can be altered, or perhaps a totally new prayer could be created.

The spiritual teacher Marianne Williamson suggests that we can adapt a current recognised prayer. In her book *A Return to Love*, she wrote about altering the end of the Christian Lord's Prayer to what felt more suitable; so instead of the usual "…for Thine is the kingdom, the power and the glory…" Marianne wrote "…for love is the kingdom, love is the power and love is the glory…"

This change of wording so resonated with me that I immediately adopted it and indeed, following her example, I made another change to the Lord's Prayer. Where one usually says, "…and deliver us from evil…" this became "…but deliver us to know and understand Thy love and grace…" as it felt more meaningful for me.

My most recently made-up prayer reflects where I am in life and I am happy to share it with you:

"Holy Mother, heavenly Father, thank you for my life. It is a good life and I have so much to be thankful for, with so much to look forward to. Thank you for helping me to find opportunities in the difficulties and challenges I have faced. I welcome you into my life and wish to learn more so I may tangibly understand your guidance and follow my spiritual path on this journey. I would not wish to take my life nor your help for granted in making it the truly wonderful life that it is."

This prayer is a combination of affirmations, cosmic ordering and gratefulness as well as a request for ongoing support.

13th August – Divination with Paint and Water

Fill a glass bowl with water and stir it a little so that it swirls very gently. Then flick some paint into it with a paintbrush (acrylic paint is good for this) and allow the paint to separate into swirls, forming shapes and outlines. When using a glass bowl it is possible to see different shapes from the side, thus providing even better imagery.

Try this as a little fun exercise in learning divination with your friends, just like reading tea leaves. Using different coloured paints will also aid the imagery. Give it a go when considering something for the future, or when focusing on a situation that needs an answer, and note what images the paint forms that can give further insights into your decision. Sometimes an image seems to appear that acts as a trigger or a reminder to entertain certain options in your decision-making, rather like Eagle energy encouraging us to consider an extended perspective of something (see the entry for 27th July).

Helpful tip: If you're not sure what to ask, try requesting, "What do I need to be aware of at this time?"

15th August – Emotional Weights

We all have negative emotions weighing on us and perhaps sometimes we don't fully appreciate how much we do carry around. Often our worst negative emotions are not voiced to anyone else, so we carry these burdens all the time. Today, let's visit a beach, or a stony riverside or waterway, and as we go along we'll collect a pebble for each negative emotion we're aware of and put them in a bag.

These emotions may be surrounding guilt, resentment, envy, annoyance, irritability, forgiveness (or lack of it), approval (or lack of it), addictions or anger towards others or ourself. Whatever the size of the issue, even if it's only minor, we pick up a pebble and put it in our bag. Bear in mind that we may also be carrying karma from previous incarnations and this baggage continues to be taken forward into our current lifetime. If we think this could be so, we should not forget to include these issues as well.

When finished, we can feel the weight of the bag and reflect on how the heavy physical weight represents the emotional weight that our spirit continuously carries around. These emotional weights can lie unresolved for years, stunting our growth, and it is far preferable to release them. So now we go to the water's edge and sit in peace for a while, looking at the number of pebbles collected. We question why these emotional weights are held onto and what doing this achieves. Are they held from a sense of martyrdom or victimhood?

Memories and emotional weights can hang around in our energetic fields even though they relate to situations long past and may no longer be relevant for us in our current conscious living. Removing these blocks helps us to step into the world a little lighter and more able to rewrite our energetic patterns, reclaiming our inner core joy and recognising that it is good to free ourselves from self-imposed conditions.

Now, one by one we take the pebbles and throw them into the water, saying something along the lines of, "I let go of (name the emotion) that is holding me back and I accept myself with love and compassion." Finally, we thank the body of water for accepting these emotions and walk away not looking back, all the while setting the intention to move forward in life.

Helpful tip: Taking further advantage of EFT (see the entry for 27th February), tap the karate chop point, the middle part of the fleshy side of the hand, when stating the intention to let go of an emotion.

17th August – Spiritual Famine

'Spiritual famine' as a root cause is important to think about at times when life does not seem to flow in its usual smooth pattern. When our lives are full and busy with work, household and family routines, we very often drop our spiritual practices. When spiritual practice forms a regular part of our lives, we feel that something is not quite right with us when they cease or diminish. If this has been happening, consider a re-engagement of spiritual practices now – even one practice a week helps the universal flow again.

We could also consider whether, if our spiritual practices have ceased, there may be another reason for this. Perhaps it's time to evaluate whether our normal practice should be allowed to lapse naturally so that another and more fulfilling one can be kindled instead, to nourish our continuing growth.

19th August – Learn to Use a Pendulum

Crystal pendulums are wonderful tools for healing work, and for general divinatory purposes a different pendulum is often used. A divinatory pendulum can easily be made from items such as a bolt tied on the end of a piece of string, a necklace or even a builder's plumb line. Let's have a go today, perhaps buying a book or planning to attend a workshop with a registered dowser to study the general divinatory actions and responses. These sessions can be fun, such as dowsing for hidden items in a room or building, and informative.

If starting out for the first time, the easiest way to figure out the 'yes' swing is to hold the length of chain or string between the forefinger and thumb so that the end weight is approximately 20 cm away from the hand. Ask the pendulum to show the 'Yes' movement and then give it a gentle swing in a straight line. After a short while the pendulum should start to move in a circulating way. When it does so, in order to check that you have understood, stop the pendulum and start again with a straight line swing and ask, "Is my name...?" The pendulum should then after a short while move as before. Do the same for the 'No' swing, except that when you want to corroborate this ask, "Am I a man/woman?" stating the opposite gender.

Pendulums can be used in many daily activities and some therapists use them to ascertain allergies, dietary choices, lifestyle habits, health issues, spiritual growth options, educational choices, questions regarding relationships and so on.

A very good instruction book on dowsing is *Dowsing for Health: the application and methods for holistic healing,* by Arthur Bailey.

Another way of using a pendulum is to allow the whole body to act as a pendulum, by standing with feet a little apart and eyes closed, becoming calm and then mentally asking questions. If the body moves forward the answer is 'Yes' and if it moves backwards the answer is 'No'; if the body wobbles or sways a little then perhaps it is not the right time to ask that particular question, or the wording is not clear enough for an answer to be given.

Helpful tip: Some people are concerned that we may energetically sway the pendulum to our own desires, so a way to guard against this is by not knowing whether the pendulum is giving a 'Yes' or 'No' answer! Use two identical pieces of paper with 'Yes' written on one and 'No' written on the other. Place these face down and shuffle them about with eyes closed. When asking a question, place the pendulum over one of the pieces and see which way it swings. When it swings positively, for example, turn over the paper to check whether 'Yes' is written there. Shuffle the two pieces of paper again before asking the next question.

21st August – Prophetic Dreams Shell

From any previous visits to a beach for collecting seashells, choose a shell for the specific purpose of asking it to help with a prophetic dream tonight. Shells are associated with many goddesses such as Doris and Danu, the ancient Gaelic goddess of water, and not forgetting Mother Mary as Stella Maris of the sea. Tonight, whisper to the shell your desire for a prophetic dream that you will remember and understand, and then place it under your pillow. The request can be for any concern, such as love, home, health or finances.

With the element of water being associated with the shell, it may be that your prophetic dream will be related to your emotions.

As mentioned in the 15th July entry about using bay and mint for prophetic dreams, the symbolism of dreams are many and varied.

However, for today let us consider the ancient history of dream interpretation and research this. Peoples the world over have been fascinated by dreams through the ages: priests, shamans and elders would often help a dreamer seeking an explanation and an interpretation. We could start our research into dream analysis and interpretation with the ancient Greeks of Hippocrates, Aristotle and Plato, or perhaps research the aboriginal Dreamtime experiences.

Sweet dreams!

23rd August – Acknowledging Trees

Our woodlands provides such grace and beauty, the trees changing through the seasons and looking especially wonderful in early summer when their leaves offer a canopy of varying shades of green.

Many people believe in tree spirits or 'dryads', who like the energy of our healing and loving thoughts being sent to them. Some are even able to connect with trees energetically and sense their feelings and the messages they wish to pass on to us. They are an ancient species of our natural world and have much wisdom.

Today, let's start a practice of acknowledging our trees, even if it's only one particular tree. Go up to it, touch it and let it know of your pleasure at its beauty and the good that it does. Your loving thoughts and acknowledgements will be appreciated. If you are able to, plant a new tree in your garden. A nice idea is to try growing an apple tree from a pip; it will not fruit, but it will grow and provide greenery for Mother Earth and a little more pleasure in our lives.

25th August – Archangel Metatron

Archangel Metatron is believed by some to have been the prophet Enoch, a celestial energy who experienced human incarnation. He is seen as a task-master, encouraging our motivation, commitment and organisation; so if these are not our usual attributes then Archangel Metatron's energy may seem rather daunting.

However, we all need prodding, urging and spurring on at times to get moving. So, when we know that we have been a little self-indulgent or lazy and some of our specific plans have been let slip, then perhaps it's time to meditate with Archangel Metatron. These summer days and the harvest period are an ideal time for us to rediscover our motivation to carry out and complete the tasks and resolutions we set ourselves during the previous winter months. Therefore, with the wheel of the year gradually moving towards autumn, a meditation with Archangel Metatron is a good thing to do now to re-attune with our commitments.

We prepare for meditation and imagine ourself in a violet bubble. There are several colours associated with Archangel Metatron, especially white, violet and sea-green, and we shall be using all three of them. Once settled, we visualise ourself in a lighthouse in the middle of the sea, knowing that it is completely safe. It is daylight with a wonderful blue sky brightness but also high winds and heavy seas. All around the lighthouse are the white peaks of high waves and the wonderful sea-green as the waves roll in.

We notice the energy and power of these waves as we imagine them crashing against our lighthouse and we use their powerful energy to inspire our own motivation. Enjoy the beauty these visions of high seas are bringing and feel the waves slough away any laziness so that there is renewed enthusiasm to embark upon our plans.

We spend some moments in our safe lighthouse and then thank Archangel Metatron for his help.

27th August – Carnelian, the Virgo Birthstone

This crystal has a jolly orange colour. It can be placed near the front door to encourage abundance and it can also help to keep other crystals cleansed. Another idea is to place it as part of a 'chakra layout' on our sacral energy centre because carnelian encourages vitality, energy and motivation as well as grounding.

Along our life path we should always be mindful of keeping ourselves grounded and in the present. Carnelian can help us to achieve this: while embracing any changes on our journey it aids our life force energy in making them, thereby providing us with the vitality to achieve.

Carnelian's sunny disposition reminds us to love life, warts and all, as this is part of our learning. So research carnelian today and buy one if possible so that it is readily available for those moments when its other qualities are required.

29th August – Our Eight-Legged Friends

It has been said that if we look at a spider and it realises we have made eye contact, the spider will stop moving. How do we put this to the test though?!

We all have hilarious (or not so funny) stories and memories of the antics of huge hairy spiders in our lives, such as seeing them racing towards us while we frantically try to move away, finding them in our bed, in our shoes and even swaying in front us while driving our cars. Some people are genuinely scared of spiders, despite knowing that those in the UK at least are completely harmless. Try to think of them as our friends, clearing areas of small insects with their intricate, clever webs. But even if we wish them no harm, we usually do not like them roaming or creating cobwebs in our living quarters.

It has also been said that we can make requests of spiders and that they listen… So today try speaking to any spiders seen in the home, asking them not to enter the living quarters and perhaps instead to remain in the porch. Maybe we could add a gentle warning that if they're found in the wrong place they'll be caught with a glass and paper and put outside! With the colder months arriving shortly, spiders will once again start entering our homes so try bearing this in mind.

Helpful tip: If you really don't like spiders in the home or car, some believe that putting horse chestnuts in likely places, or in the four corners of a room, keeps them away.

31st August – What's Your Learning Style?

In recent years it has been acknowledged that many people feel a barrier to learning; for example, dyslexia has made them give up any form of activity involving the written word. But this can deny us great achievements. One only has to think of Helen Keller and wonder what we would have missed in life without her example. And we should applaud her governess who did not give up trying to teach her a sign language that could be understood by someone who was blind, deaf and of impeded speech.

We should all consider what our particular learning style is, or for that matter styles, as many of us will have a balance of different methods. Some thrive on auditory learning, lecture hall style, some like reading, others prefer hands-on or kinaesthetic methods even without the need for a manual while others cope better visually. Visual people like to observe, preferring diagrams, displays, hand-outs and films; when unsure of something they will probably want a demonstration. Auditory people prefer the spoken word and often say "Tell me…" in conversation. Kinaesthetic people like a practical approach with a "Let me try…" attitude.

During infant schooldays, activity is combined with other learning methods, creating a balance that is usually helpful for our understanding as the usual milestones are achieved. However, as we grow and schooling becomes more studious, the formal style can be a struggle for some people who may not be suited to it.

Today, let's reflect back on our school or college days. Were any stages especially easy or difficult and was this because of how things were taught and what was involved in the teaching? These reflections may be important for our own ongoing learning or for the development of other family members who may be struggling. For example, let's imagine that we're going to run a training course for work colleagues or even an informal session with friends; we'd be wise to incorporate visual, auditory and kinaesthetic aspects into our teaching so there'd be a chance that one or a balance of all three learning styles would suit them and they could make progress.

It is also recognised that there are several distinct personality types in the approach to learning new skills or facing challenges. For example, the 'activist' is open-minded and can fully involve themselves, while 'reflectors' prefer to stand back from a situation and observe from different angles before they take any action; 'theorists' deal with things in a logical way, being objective and using their analytical skills, but 'pragmatists' prefer finding practical solutions to problems.

If we can be more aware of our own personal learning styles in different kinds of situation, it can help us make better choices and decisions.

Helpful tip: The energetic vibrations of malachite, sugilite and tourmaline are said to help with dyslexia so this may be worth researching further if it's relevant for you or someone you know.

September

September is a time of new routines, children returning to school, the lighter evenings noticeably reducing. Fruit berries are harvested and perhaps we can see some of the results of our own plans made during last winter coming to fruition. September can also see us revelling in our accomplishments and acknowledging our experiences and learning, once again being grateful for these as well as for the food harvests. The autumn equinox, also known as Mabon, is in September and is a time when Mother Earth starts donning her winter mantle in preparation for nature's hibernation.

1st September – Demeter

This ancient Greek goddess of the harvest was also petitioned to restore and improve health with her love and kindness. Today, let us pay respect to the goddess Demeter by making sandwiches to reflect gratitude for the wheat harvest and then cut them in the shape of a heart to represent pure love from the heart. When doing so, we acknowledge the goddess Demeter's part in our lives through the ages, for the harvests occurring all over the world every year.

Helpful tip: Whole wheat and whole grain bread contain vitamin E and fibre which are important for our health, so let's use this when making our sandwiches.

3rd September – A Four Elements Balanced Home

A balanced and harmonious home can be achieved in several ways, such as with Feng Shui or crystals. However, the natural elements of fire, air, earth and water can also play a part in maintaining a harmonious balance. Try giving this a go today as it is very easy to achieve.

The elements of earth and water can be introduced simply by having a few plants placed in each room. Fire is achieved by lighting candles, or a fire in your hearth or wood burner in the colder months. For the air, we should ensure there is always a window open when we're at home; if we go out then on returning we can open a window, allowing any stagnant air to escape and fresh, energetic air to enter the home.

Homes or workplaces where very little fresh air has been allowed to circulate can have an atmosphere that seems stale or heavy, as if the energy has become dense and stuck, so allowing in fresh air is important. Start balancing your home today with these four elements and monitor any subtle differences.

Helpful tip: It is possible to buy bamboo shoots in water as part of Feng Shui practice so one of these would fulfil the earth and water elements and be auspicious at the same time.

5th September – Nelson Mandela

On the morning Nelson Mandela died, a beautiful trio of swans flew overhead as a few of us conducted a 'prayers to the Earth' routine on the front lawn of our offices before we started our working day. We had decided beforehand to dedicate our few minutes of peaceful mindfulness to the memory of Nelson Mandela and to his personal attribute of not giving up in his fight for social justice. Despite his incarceration for many years, his qualities enabled a country to reconcile and he showed the world this possibility as a shining beacon.

Swans had never flown over us before, nor since, during our routine. The delicate sound of their wings gracefully forging through the air above us was an incredible experience and all of us finished the routine with tearful eyes at what had occurred.

If we look at Swan in the Celtic animal calendar (2nd – 29th Sept), it denotes spiritually evolved and high standards. A good description of Nelson Mandela? From today, let's all try harder to incorporate his qualities into our lives and try to soar gracefully like the swans.

7th September – Courage Stones

Try to find some small stones today, preferably with a smooth surface on one side. At home, prepare a list of motivational words such as courage, strength, determination, commitment, passion, willpower, energy, focus, confidence, bravery and so on.

Then on the following Tuesday, because this day is ruled by Mars who gives us strength, mark on the pebbles in felt tip or paint the above example words or other meaningful ones, even a short phrase if there's room. A single initial letter will do if the stones are small, as long as you know what it represents. Once done, spend a little quiet time contemplating how these characteristics can be achieved and maintained.

Choose a pebble to carry in your pocket for a week and occasion-ally allow it to help with your focus on that particular characteristic. Then on the following Tuesday spend a few moments contemplating your achievements during the previous week before choosing another courage stone with a different characteristic to work with for the ensuing week.

Continue this practice every Tuesday for as long as you feel it is necessary, all the while being grateful for the positive changes and for the journey of learning. It can occasionally feel daunting when we seek the courage or determination we need in our lives but facing our challenges can engender salutary experiences and bring positive changes to our lives.

Helpful tip: Strength and Mars are linked with the colour red so, if the stones are lightly coloured, using red ink for the words will also provide the energetic vibration of strength for your courage to grow.

9th September – Asking for Help

Today let's think about asking for help from the universe, from the spirit world, from the angels or our guides, from our higher selves, from the gods and goddesses according to our beliefs. If we can acknowledge that it is a kind and friendly universe, and there are kind and friendly energies looking after our wellbeing, then why not ask them for help? Many spiritual leaders tell us that higher beings wish to help us and all we need to do is ask them. So come on, let's ask help for our healing, for healing of others or guidance in certain matters.

This is not about us becoming reliant upon this way of thinking and relinquishing any of our own responsibility for our lives. It is about us doing our best to deal with practical issues, trying to apply our wisdom to challenges and decisions, but recognising that there are times when we need extra help and that the universal energies can give it.

If we're about to walk up a steep hillside, we can ask the angels to help with a boost of energy. If mulling over a certain issue to find a way forward, we could ask our higher self and guides to help us during the night so the matter can be dealt with better on waking the next morning. If some aspect of home decorating or renovation is not going according to plan, we can ask help from the spirit world, perhaps focusing on a family member who has passed on and who was good at DIY. If we need help in connecting with an animal, we ask an animal guide or the archangel Ariel. If an item is lost, the archangel Chamuel can provide the inspiration to know where to look.

It's not necessary to perform any ritualistic ceremony when asking for help. We just plainly say, with sincerity, "Please can you help me with…?" The universal energies know what help is needed so, if we limit the request with overly precise wording, the help the universe is able to offer is also limited.

Think about this today. We are not on our own. Spiritual and celestial energies are willing to help us, so we just have to ask them – and say a quiet 'Thank you' afterwards!

Helpful tip: Bear in mind that when we are sincere in our requests, the universe brings us what we need. This may not always be what we thought it would be!

11ᵗʰ September – Reading Tea Leaves

This is an enjoyable activity that can be carried out alone with each morning's beverage or perhaps with a group of friends. Tea leaves or coffee grains can be used and the shapes they leave behind in the cup can often suggest something relevant for an issue we're involved with or reflect our current thoughts.

You could have some light-hearted fun with friends today and try reading each other's tea leaf remains in the cups. One drinks most of the liquid leaving only a small amount with the leaves, which is then swirled three times clockwise before the cup is up-ended onto the saucer ready for the leaves to be read by another person in the group. If anyone doesn't actually like tea, they can still hold the cup in both hands for a while so their energy is naturally imprinting itself; then after about five minutes most of the liquid is poured away before following the routine above.

Usually, several images and shapes can be seen but on some occasions all that can be seen is just one big picture. We should always say what is seen, however silly, as it may resonate with the person who drank the tea.

For ongoing practice, whenever we're in a busy café and the table still has to be cleared by the staff, try looking into the leftover cups and mugs and see if there are any outlines from the grains or frothy milk on the inside as this helps to hone our skills when searching for outlines.

Helpful tip: If you like this form of divination, called tasseomancy, and want to take it further, purchase a book that provides more detailed information such as where the leaf picture is located within the cup, which can suggest a timeline. These books generally include lists of what various outlines portend, although some people simply prefer to use their own intuition.

13th September – Healing Thoughts

Purchase a light blue candle today as this colour is associated with healing. If possible, also try to source an amethyst pyramid crystal to work alongside the blue candle for when you wish to send healing thoughts for others. The pyramid shape has long been thought to emit a powerful energy and this can be harnessed for healing intentions. Amethyst has healing qualities itself, recognised by the ancients.

Once prepared and ready to send healing wishes for someone, light the candle and state the healing request aloud. Write the name of the person on a piece of paper, or use a photograph if available, and place it beside the candle while focusing on sending healing thoughts. If you do have an amethyst pyramid then place the photograph or piece of paper under the crystal.

Helpful tip: If the intention is to keep a large blue pillar candle just for healing purposes, then consider anointing it with water from a holy well (see the entry for 1ˢᵗ February). Further, the caduceus – a sword with two snakes intertwined – is a sign known as the healing wand and this could be carved into the candle for added power.

15ᵗʰ September – Apples and Aphrodite

Apple blossom has a beautiful aroma and is regarded by Celtic people as a symbol of love. The ensuing fruit were also considered sacred to Aphrodite, the Greek goddess of love. To celebrate the apple harvest at this time and its links to Aphrodite, let's cook something today with apples and express grateful thanks to the Earth for this blessed fruit.

Many children like toffee apples so we could perhaps consider making toffee apples instead and join in with the young ones, allowing our inner child to surface.

Apples are recognised to have many health benefits, recognised in the well-known phrase 'An apple a day keeps the doctor away'. In fact apples contain anti-oxidants and aid our heart health, also helping to control diabetes.

17ᵗʰ September – St Hildegard of Bingen

This Christian mystic from Germany experienced visions from a young age and eventually became a Benedictine nun, subsequently an abbess. She died at the age of 81 years on 17ᵗʰ September, 1179, which is now her feast day. St Hildegard was a prolific writer, including songs and poems, and indeed it is felt by some that she produced some of the most beautiful music still being sung by choristers today.

St Hildegard had a holistic approach to healing, such as recommending boiling water before drinking it in order to prevent infection, sowing seeds on a waxing moon and suggesting that the waxing moon was also a good time for human conception. Her two tomes of healing practices are known as *The Physica* and *Causae et Curae*. Some people today continue farming according to the moon's cycle, thus planting, sowing and harvesting in accordance with the waxing and waning phases; books are printed with moon phases and timings for guidance.

St Hildegard's holistic health practices were during a period when the Cathars in France were being persecuted by the Roman Catholic Church, subsequently leading to the Inquisition in later years, so perhaps we are blessed to have access to her wisdom. Throughout many European countries these practices went underground for fear of reprisals from the Church and therefore we may have lost many pearls of wisdom, not only from St Hildegard but from other healers of the monasteries and abbeys who were at risk.

Look up some of St Hildegard's writings, songs or poems today to see if any of them resonate with your own interests.

Helpful tip: Biodynamic farming, based on Rudolf Steiner's theories from the 1920s, is an approach being observed by some farmers today which also works in conjunction with the moon's phases to take advantage of its influences for the growth and nurture of livestock as well as crops. You may like to research this on the Internet to compare these natural practices with those of our forebears.

19th September – Honouring Wild Food

Wild food walks are very popular now and take place on a regular basis in many parts of the country, with a plethora of books also available advising on foraging. The simplest and commonest of wild food collecting is the usual blackberry picking time in late August and September each year.

Elderberries can also be harvested each September to make a winter cordial to drink as an excellent immune booster. This is achieved by simmering the elderberries for approximately thirty minutes with Echinacea and cinnamon. Pour the mixture through muslin into a jug or container and as it cools add local honey to the cordial. An easy way to make this in a batch is to pour the cordial mixture into ice cube trays and then freeze it. When winter arrives and we feel in need of an extra boost for our health, just pop an elderberry cordial ice cube into a mug and pour hot water over it ready to drink.

When foraging, please be mindful that the fruits of a living energy are being harvested so we should express thanks for the food that the trees and plants have provided, whether they are cultivated berries and herbs from our garden or on wild foraging treks. Take care, too, that what you are picking is not poisonous!

Respecting Mother Earth for her bounty and honouring the nutritious food she provides for us is an important ritual in our lives. Our minds are enriched by the beauty of these plants and our bodies are enriched by their nutritious sustenance, so let's start a practice of honouring these plants and being grateful for their wonderful foods when we harvest them.

Helpful tip: Read Jo Dunbar's *The Spirit of the Hedgerow* as a guide to the medicinal properties of our native plants as well as for fascinating descriptions of the folklore associated with them.

21ˢᵗ September – The Autumn Equinox

The spring and autumn equinoxes are linked with balance, times when night and day are of equal length. Let us take a little time to look at our wardrobes of clothes. Check the colours and note whether there is an imbalance of black, grey, brown, navy and generally dark colours rather than soft and warming pastel colours with bright splashes of colour amongst them. Colour has its own vibration and this would be a good time to check out the basic colour meanings.

The colder winter months will shortly arrive and it would be complementary to our health to wear balanced clothing during this time as an aid to our body's general function. We should think about the yin and yang of balance and harmony and adopt this for the colour vibrations of our clothes for beneficial health. Investigating colour therapy can also assist in deciding whether to abandon some clothing colours altogether or amalgamate colours that would not usually be adopted.

We could consider a range of 'chakra-coloured' clothing to help with the energetic vibration of particular energy centres such as a blue scarf for the throat to enable improved communication, a pair of red boots for energy when out walking, an orange jumper to wear on gloomy winter days and for when we wish to express our inner child, and a green jumper to wear in preparation for a potentially stressful day so that the heart centre remains peaceful and calm. Perhaps we could even purchase a purple hat as this colour is good for when meditating outside due to its association with the spiritual, intuitive and mystical parts of us, linked to the crown chakra.

Have fun with the colours! Enjoy them and feel good in what is being worn, knowing that they also complement our health and help to provide us with a sense of balance.

23rd September – Dancing

In recognition of World Alzheimer's Day recently, try dancing. It doesn't matter what style of dance: ballroom, salsa, disco, line dancing or folk. Why dance? An American study has shown that dancing frequently is 76% more likely to keep our minds and cognitive processes functioning healthily. We may think we have it covered by completing crosswords or other puzzles; however, dancing is up to 29% better than puzzles.

The dementia care team in a certain area of Cornwall, for example, regularly organise tea dances at a local hotel where the older generation can get on the dance floor and 'strut their stuff'. The sparkle in their eyes and the enjoyment on their faces are great to witness, even though some are in wheelchairs and only able to watch. So no matter what your age, put on your dancing shoes today!

25th September – Making a Corn Cage

Beautifully intricate corn dollies are traditionally made to represent the spirit of the corn and to express gratitude for the grain harvest. Whilst they are pleasing to look at, they can be difficult to create if one is not skilled in this craft. A far simpler activity to celebrate this time of Mabon is with a corn cage.

Firstly, cut out some thick card into any shape such as a circle, square or heart and cut holes around the outline. Then push straw stems through and anchor them underneath with sticky tape. Just underneath the heads of the grain, tie the straw stems together with a ribbon; but before doing so, whisper your wishes for the next six months into the corn cage. The corn cage is thus able to stand on a shelf.

The ribbon colour used can be linked with its energetic vibration. For example, red is for protection, strength, passion, courage, vitality and willpower. Green is for money, fertility, growth, abundance, luck and employment. Blue represents healing, patience, harmony and communication. Yellow is for intellect, study, divination, friendship and creativity. Gold is used for happiness, success, prosperity and career matters and purple is for wisdom, spiritual love, honour, psychic ability and business.

For added power, three coloured ribbons could be plaited together. Keep the corn cage until the spring equinox when it can be burned on the last hearth fire or in the garden, at the same time thanking the universe for its benevolence towards your wishes during the previous six month period.

Helpful tip: The best straw to use for aesthetic purposes is barley as it produces an elegant display with its particular grain head.

27ᵗʰ September – Justice

The major arcana card of Justice in the Tarot is linked to Libra and concerns judgement of our own behaviours and actions. It encourages us to reflect upon whether we have been honourable. Have our motives, actions and behaviours been honourable? This is about being honourable to ourselves as well as towards others.

If on reflection we consider that there were times when we fell short, we should not berate ourselves but simply acknowledge these experiences as being in the past and choose to learn from them instead. It is not possible to change what happened. In any case, our reflection is our own particular story and others involved may not see things the same way at all and could wonder what all the fuss is about. Therefore, our illusory thoughts can stop us from finding peace.

Behaving honourably is believed by some as a matter of 'karmic law' in that good, honourable intentions and actions create good karma in our lives now and for our next incarnation. During reflection, we should consider whether other avenues or courses of action could have been undertaken and use this exercise as guidance for the future.

Saint Teresa of Calcutta said, "God does not command that we do great things, only little things with great love." Perhaps this phrase can be our springboard for change if the Justice card has resonated with our reflections, helping us to plan for honourable intentions in the future.

29th September – Archangel Jophiel

Rich golden yellow is the colour of Archangel Jophiel. She represents wisdom and illumination and in accepting these qualities into our lives we aid our life's journey and spiritual growth.

The colour yellow is linked with the solar plexus chakra. When we make a wrong choice in our decisions or actions, leading us down a path that is not in our best interests, the wisdom of our higher selves know this and it is reflected in our solar plexus becoming jittery. Once we understand why our solar plexus is behaving in this way, we can use our wisdom to change and so bring peace to this chakra centre.

Let's take some time today for meditation and visualise sitting in a rich golden yellow bubble. We sense feeling at peace with ourself and that the beautiful yellow rose, also called Peace, is in a bud formation in the solar plexus. Then we watch it gradually unfurl its petals, opening to a wide flower head. From within the centre of this yellow rose, miniscule pollen powder gently floats around, permeating our solar plexus area then spreading out to the other chakras where it settles upon all our organs, bones, muscles and blood cells, creating peace wherever the golden yellow pollen lands.

Next we imagine the golden yellow pollen spreading outside the body, spiralling and gently dusting golden yellow pollen all over. We visualise it floating elegantly in our energy fields, suffusing peace as a comforting blanket, as we allow this peaceful feeling to let in spiritual love throughout our whole being, for this love brings us wisdom and understanding.

To finish, close the yellow rose to a bud once again and thank Archangel Jophiel for her help in sending spiritual peace and love.

October

The crone goddess is now evident. Chilly mornings and evenings. The first frosts. The light is definitely decreasing and we now enter the period of the dark of the year. There are preparations for forthcoming Samhain and the new wheel of the year, heart-warming foods and globe thistles drying out ready for decorations at Christmas.

1st October – A Walking Chant

When the aborigines of Australia go 'walkabout' they are walking the paths, and probably ley lines, of their ancient forebears and while walking these paths they sing to the land they travel along. And as they conduct their sacred Dreamtime ceremonies, special paths are used while also singing to the land. What a wonderful and worthy practice to adopt, that of the land being healed and honoured by generations. Our countryside is accessible with hundreds of public footpaths for us to try this.

As each foot is placed on the ground, imagine that you intend sending an energy wave of healing thoughts in honour of Mother Earth. She continues to nurture us despite our treatment towards her, so this would be an opportunity for us to manifest healing for her as well as expressing our gratitude.

Choose a song or chant with a gentle tune so that the practice is meditative and soothing. If not able to walk in the countryside, perhaps visit your local park, waterway or beach.

Helpful tip: If unsure what to chant or sing then try chanting 'OM' as it resembles the sound of the universe and will resonate with the Earth.

3rd October – A Written Mandala

Mandalas have become very popular recently and it is now possible to buy colouring books with mandala outlines printed in preparation for individual colouring. Some find fulfilment of their creative desires with this and focusing upon the colours in a beautiful pattern is an easy example of meditative and calming mindfulness in our everyday lives.

However, there is another mandala option that could be tried, using the written word. All that is needed is a piece of paper and a round saucer as an outline of the starting point. Think of a word or phrase to use as a mantra each day, such as 'My life is full of love and compassion' or simply 'Peace'. Start on the outside of the circle repeatedly writing this phrase as a continuous piece of writing around the circle. When nearing the starting point gently alter the flow of writing so that it carries on under the first circle outline and keep on writing the phrase or word in an ever-decreasing circle until arriving at the centre.

The mantra can be general but equally it can be as specific as we wish, used as a good reminder. An example could be the phrase "I am strong" if a big challenge is coming up, such as expecting the return of someone into our lives who was previously an 'energy vampire' and we do not wish to return to that particular type of friendship. This mandala would serve as a gentle reminder for us to be mindful in a potential situation and to be strong in resisting a return to an old pattern.

Try this today. Be adventurous in your use of colour too with different pens and gels or using different coloured paper. This is also an activity that can be done with children.

Helpful tip: If unsure about the wording of your mandala, perhaps try a little meditation beforehand as calming the mind often allows our intuition and insight to register with our conscious mind and a phrase or word may come to the fore.

5th October – The Celtic Animal Sign of Butterfly (30th Sept – 27th Oct)

'Social butterflies' seen at parties are cheerful, bright and uplifting people who make friends and acquaintances quite happily and easily; at times perhaps we have wished ourselves to be able to behave similarly. Butterfly in terms of symbolism is about transformation, breaking out from our cocoons and flying freely, becoming the person we wish to be regardless of how small or great the transformation.

It is now time for us to consider whether there is anything we wish to transform in our lives and, if so, to start making and preparing our plans for how we can achieve them over the pending winter months. Then, in line with the Earth's cycle, we shall set these free in early spring next year.

For example, perhaps attending assertiveness classes at the local evening education establishment may help us in overcoming shyness, or learning a foreign language will transform our career opportunities, enabling a job relocation abroad. Learning to drive a car to widen our horizons in many areas could also be an option to consider.

Whatever we decide upon to help transform our lives, let's always be mindful of the butterfly – bright, cheerful and uplifting – and the universe will respond, flowing abundantly and assisting in our transformation.

Helpful tip: Transforming ourselves can sometimes take a lot of courage in taking that first step on the path to a new way of living. Crystals to consider using when undertaking changes are ametrine, labradorite, malachite and muscovite. Flower remedies can also help.

7th October – Herbal Remedies

Our ancient forebears used herbalism widely and traditions vary throughout the world, such as western, TCM (Traditional Chinese Medicine), Arabic and Ayurveda. The most famous western herbalist was Nicholas Culpeper and his original text *Culpeper's Complete Herbal* from 1653 is still used as a source of information for our current day herbalists. Monasteries and priories grew their own medicinal or physic gardens for use in treating the ailments of their local population, such as garlic and Echinacea for abscesses, lobelia for asthma, chamomile for anxiety, peppermint for catarrh, angelica for colic, valerian for cramp and feverfew for headaches. Some restrictions apply in their use today and it is important for a qualified herbalist to be consulted in certain matters.

Health food shops in the High Street offer a huge range of herbal remedies, and there are some self-help books available for those who wish to practise simple remedies for general wellbeing. Examples could be the smothering of cayenne pepper over toes suffering from chilblains, an extremely quick and inexpensive remedy, incorporating garlic in our meals as a general wellbeing food that boosts our immune system, and gathering nettles from our gardens or organic hedgerows to immerse in soups for their high vitamin C content.

Many gardeners use the natural fertilising benefits of the comfrey plant by soaking its leaves in water and using this diluted as a liquid fertiliser. However, the old folk called this plant by the common name of knitbone as it did exactly that, helped to knit broken bones together. This plant can also be used for arthritic and rheumatic aches in our joints by macerating it in organic cold-pressed olive oil for a 28-day moon cycle, sieving, then warming gently and melting in beeswax ready for an ointment. Two drops each of camomile and lavender essential oils into the mixture also help with the aroma of the comfrey ointment.

The NHS was formed in 1948 as a means of preventing illness and diseases but unfortunately its emphasis has appeared to alter from prevention to treatment. So consider taking over some of your own health prevention from today and create some simple herbal remedy routines. Perhaps you could plan to grow your own physic garden next year.

Helpful tip: Research and plan a visit to a physic garden as there is much that can be learned. Some monastic communities still maintain their physic garden, such as Buckfast Abbey in Devon.

9th October – Volunteering

Giving of our time, love, effort and energy in caring for others and the environment is a wonderful way of bringing our own energy fields into balance. When we feel good in ourselves about what we are doing to help others, this in turn has a knock-on effect with our aura. Being physically active, mentally stimulated and finding comradeship and esprit de corps with our fellow volunteers also creates a whole wellbeing reaction for our bodies and energy fields.

There are many outlets for volunteering such as joining the clean-up of a local beach or river, helping out in a charity shop, doing a charity fun run, being a dog-walker at our local rescue centre or a hospital visitor... the list is endless. The sense of achievement when volunteering can improve our self-esteem no end and at the same time be humbling when we consider the situation we're involved in: humbled at the sight of a beautiful river or pond, humbled by people suffering in hospitals or hospices exhibiting great bravery, humbled when people who have little themselves continue to give for the benefit of others.

Volunteering helps us to learn in so many ways and especially in learning to love and care; this is a spiritual practice in itself and some would say it is the only spiritual practice to foster. Volunteering our time, effort and love is a wonderful action benefiting others and ourselves at the same time. So today let's consider this as a possible activity for the future, whether as a regular session or just a one-off project.

11th October – A Protective Bubble for Animals

When driving along our roads, especially in the countryside, we can be saddened to see animals that have suffered traffic trauma lying in the roadside. From today, let's start a practice of placing any animal seen along our roads (cats, dogs, birds, rabbits, foxes, or even larger ones such as badgers or deer) in a protective bubble and ask Archangel Ariel to keep these beloved creatures safe. Animals enrich our lives, whether as our domestic pets or as wildlife, and with all of us playing our little part in their protection it is a kind and loving energy sent from us for them.

Helpful tip: A short prayer could be memorised for this or Reiki healers could perhaps superimpose over the animal a Reiki symbol for its healing.

13th October – A Letterbox Charm

Letterbox charms make lovely gifts for others as they are so simple to make but have thought in their preparation. Crystals have beautiful energies and making a letterbox charm using jade for good luck, with carnelian as a continuous cleanser of the jade, could be the perfect token gift for family and friends, perhaps even a Christmas gift for neighbours.

Place the two crystals in a small pouch of green or gold and let the recipient of the gift know to place it in their post box or hang it by their letterbox. We all like abundance in our lives so spread some in the lives of people we cherish.

15th October – A Ghost Walk

Ghost walks or tours can be such fun and, if one is organised in your local area, memories of unusual events or interesting stories may arise, bringing a smile. When I was young, I frequently entered an old Methodist church that had been turned into a hall; its basement toilets were said to be haunted and one evening a friend and I were locked in there by 'something' until we were rescued. This old building was later demolished and a large shop built on the site; however, several shop workers say that the basement store room is haunted and that's probably where the old toilets were located!

Ghost walks take place in many towns and cities and have become very popular in recent times. Have fun today and check out booking a tour with family or friends. But be discerning too and ensure that a tour is chosen that as well as being fun and informative is also reputable. Of special interest would be a ghost tour in an old city such as London or York, or even Paris could be considered if willing to travel further.

17th October – Death in the Tarot

In the Tarot, the major arcana card of Death is linked with the astrological sign of Scorpio. The Death card is about endings of course but also new beginnings. It represents an opportunity for transformation by cutting our ties to old patterns no longer relevant in our lives, saying cheerio to outmoded habits and addictions, in order to make way for renewal and enabling us to come out the other side liberated and in a better position to accept the universal flow of life.

If we continue to fill our lives with the 'same old same old' and we stagnate, it is difficult to make space for new, exciting and worthy energies to enter our lives.

So let's spend a little time today considering which habits, addictions and patterns we maintain that stop us from accepting transformation, and make a resolution to deal with them – practically, emotionally and spiritually – to allow renewal to commence. Our reflections may highlight several things to release but it is important that we are not overwhelmed by trying to deal with them all at once, as then we can lose heart and our motivation dissolves.

Yet one small change begets another change and we may find that working through each one in turn will generally improve the whole; the end parts of our list may gradually disappear as they are no longer valid. Often, habits and relationship patterns depend on one another to keep their momentum, so gradually removing them one by one naturally allows other outmoded habits and patterns to lift from our lives.

19th October – Ivy Month (30th Sept – 27th Oct)

This is an appropriate time, with the grain and fruit harvests almost complete, to be grateful for all the blessings we have in life.

In order to make this a little fun, why not play a game of catching falling leaves near some trees and each time a falling leaf is caught say a 'thank you' for a particular blessing. When we go with family or friends to a local wood and take a picnic, this makes a pleasant and fun event. It is good to be out in the countryside, and running or moving quickly to catch a leaf before it drops also helps to exercise us and keep us warm if the day is chilly.

Being genuinely grateful in our lives as a regular practice can become an anchoring mainstay for our character and when this positive energy is genuinely expressed from us the universe is also grateful.

21st October – An Ancestor Altar

Permanent ancestor altars in our homes can be situated on a wall shelf or on top of a bookcase. They are generally not recognised for what they are by visitors as they will probably include photographs of family members, a candle, perhaps a figurine denoting spiritual energy and a vase of the favourite flowers of someone in the spirit world.

So they could be seen as simply a display of family photographs. However, these altars are focal points for when we wish to honour and offer our grateful thanks to our ancestors and forebears. Our cherished memories of routine family life as well as the special occasions when we gathered together should be thought of as sacred, being based on spiritual qualities of love and joy.

The altar is a reminder of how the loving bonds of family pass through the generations, acting as a reassurance and motivation to continue in the same vein for the new generations. Equally, if memories have not been so good, it is a focal point for forgiveness.

Today, consider whether a permanent ancestor altar can be created in your home and allow it to help reinforce the loving bonds of generations.

23rd October – Spending Time with Others

We spend our time with family, friends, work colleagues, perhaps the general public in our work and with acquaintances during our leisure pastimes. However, sometimes we find that time spent with certain people drains or exhausts us. Perhaps we attend leisure activities and find that instead of feeling uplifted and re-energised we feel the opposite, or we may have a sinking feeling when meeting up with a certain person or group of people.

If so then perhaps it is time for us to delve into these feelings and senses to decipher what lies behind them.

We should consider whether there's one person within our leisure group who is causing a disruption or whether perhaps it is the building itself, or the activity no longer suits our desires. It may be possible that our work clients suck our energy or there's a work colleague with whom it seems impossible to get along. We may feel that some of our friends are always taking from us or perhaps family members are forever bickering or misinterpreting conversations.

If any of these sound familiar then maybe we should take some action: stopping our friends from always taking by not always giving, setting our boundaries more firmly and not being a people pleaser. We should learn to protect our energy field so that clients cannot drain us, and visualise a difficult work colleague in a pink bubble of compassion. Maybe it is time to change our leisure activities if our current ones no longer suit us, or consider switching activities to another location if we think that 'sick-building syndrome' is pertinent – sometimes geopathic stress can affect a building, caused by several factors including stagnant water underground with its negative energies permeating the building.

When we think about our companions in life and consider whether we have chosen wisely in creating friendships with them, it's worth remembering that sometimes people enter and play a particular role in our lives for a good reason, some for a long time and some only briefly, in order to help us learn important life lessons. We all want companionship with others to be harmonious, joyful and meaningful; but we should also recognise that every relationship can offer opportunities for our personal growth and even a difficult friend may be a teacher in some respect. Being respectful and sensible in our reflections will help us to make wise changes.

Helpful tip: Gridding rose quartz crystals around our home for their energies of love and compassion to permeate the family home and ease tensions may be helpful (see the entry for 3rd February).

25th October – Shamanism

Shamans honour and respect spirits in all life: animals, birds, plants, trees, the air, water and of course the Earth itself. The shaman works with nature as part of everyday living. They conduct healing ceremonies and can journey to other realms of the subconscious to help retrieve part of a person's injured soul that has fragmented (believing this to be a cause of illness or misfortune) and do so with the help of their power animals. A power animal can be a bear, wolf, eagle, panther or other more humble species relevant to their country.

Today, check out Shamanism to gain a little understanding of this wonderful path. Shamans are known by other names depending on the traditions of their country, such as the Sangoma in Africa. Each tradition has their own 'tools of the trade' to work with such as plants indigenous to their area and various divinatory tools such as bones, stones and shells.

Helpful tip: *Singing the Soul Back Home: Shamanic wisdom for every day,* by Caitlin Matthews, may provide a good introduction to understanding Shamanism as well as offering some practical exercises.

27th October – Reed Month (28th Oct – 24th Nov)

This month is a good time to think about and plan for our future year, especially if our achievements thus far have enabled us to grow and we have a desire to expand this further in the next year.

Sometimes, though, specifically making plans can seem too onerous. Therefore, find a quiet moment and simply daydream today. Sit in comfort and look out of the window or if you have a special place such as a beach, riverside or the top of a hill, then take a flask and allow the special surroundings to offer their support in this exercise.

You could create a cairn using any stones in the area if possible, a calming activity for the mind. It may be surprising what arises and can be taken forward. Make a note of any thoughts or ideas in your spiritual journal as a gentle reminder to be considered when appropriate.

29th October – Decorate a Broomstick

Many of us have seen small broomsticks for sale in the supermarkets as we near Hallowe'en, for use when children dress up as witches, with the array of fancy dress at this time now being huge and varied.

Let's buy a mini-broomstick today and appeal to our inner child for some playfulness in decorating it with sticky stars and crescent moons, ribbons, flowers and feathers. We can have some fun with our children or grandchildren as well.

When completed it could be placed as a 'notice' in the front window, to indicate there being bowls of sweets for the trick-or-treaters calling later. It could then be given away to the last caller as an additional treat, or after Hallowe'en we could perhaps hang the broomstick above the front door inside the home as a welcome sign to visitors.

31st October – A Samhain Meditation

Samhain is pronounced 'sow-wen' and otherwise known as Hallowe'en, a time to connect with our ancestors. If trick-or-treaters are likely to call then either wait until later in the evening or do this earlier in the day, perhaps even on waking. Be near your ancestor altar if possible (see 21st October), otherwise place items representing them nearby.

Light some candles, close the eyes and visualise any passed over family members. Let them know you are sending love and peace to them and that you thank them in turn for the love and support they lend from the spirit world. If you know that a family member passed over with an illness, send your loving thoughts to them for healing their spirit and request them in turn to spread that healing balm to the family on Earth so that any fears they have can be assuaged.

Be thoughtful and thankful to them and express your gratitude for all they did. Generally, people do the best they can for their family according to what is possible for them at the time; we all have our limitations and today's social restrictions are also vastly different from those in the past when there was less freedom of choice. Therefore, we should reflect on the issue of forgiveness and, if we feel able, send loving thoughts so that these sorts of wounds can also heal throughout the family.

Think of the fun times too, of course, the laughter, the family gatherings such as weddings, and recall your cherished moments with those who have passed on, thanking and blessing them. Request their ongoing love from the spirit world, lending their guidance when it's needed. Perhaps we could request that they make themselves known when they are near, such as by a gentle waft of grandmother's favourite perfume or the smell of a tobacco pouch if grandfather smoked a pipe. Whilst we may trust in the spirit world, sometimes it is good to receive tangible evidence that their love and support are nearby at difficult times in our lives.

November

Frosty mornings. Bracing walks in blustery winds. Warm coats, scarves, woolly hats and mittens. Log fires and warming mugs of hot chocolate. Thanksgiving. Peaceful reflection and planning. Natural hibernation!

1ˢᵗ **November – Soul Cakes**

Today is All Saints Day and tomorrow is known as All Souls Day. Soul cakes were baked in years gone by and given to the poor and hungry as a form of alms. As a way of expressing gratitude for our own gifts and blessings of abundance, maybe we could bake some soul cakes today and take them to work tomorrow with a request for donations to a local homeless charity. Or we could give them to elderly or infirm neighbours. This would be a modern example of alms.

Also today make a plan for next month that, if working, instead of our work colleagues or personal contacts sending Christmas cards to each other, we each donate food items into a central box to be delivered to the local food bank for the Christmas distribution.

Here is a guide of the ingredients needed for soul cakes: 375 g of self-raising flour, ½ teaspoon of salt, 155 g of caster sugar, 90 g of currants, 90 g of sultanas, 1 egg, 125 ml of milk, 185 g of butter, 2 teaspoons of nutmeg, 2 teaspoons of mixed spice, 1 teaspoon of cinnamon and 1 teaspoon of ginger. The method is easily found online.

3ʳᵈ **November – Photographing Orbs**

This is a phenomenon that often appears on photographs especially in recent times. An orb is usually a small sphere of white light, although other colours are possible, and many believe that they are spiritual energies in the atmosphere around us all the time. Whatever the truth is of this, they are intriguing. With the digital photography age it has become possible to photograph orbs and other unusual phenomenon quite easily with our cameras or mobile phones.

Try this twice today, once during daylight and the second time during the dark evening. Beforehand each time, spend a few moments in peace and calm before quietly stating your intentions and requesting your guardian angel or guides to assist. This offers a sort of prior notice or invitation to the spirit world that enables them to pay a visit.

Then take a variety of images, some in the home and some outdoors, hopefully capturing any visiting energies. For the evening session, try this near trees if possible and take photographs around their energies. It may be possible to capture unusual outlines as well as orbs.

Helpful tip: Both of these sessions may yield better results if you're with a group of like-minded friends, as your combined energies and requests may help to raise the energy required for the orbs to appear. Further, Jaap Rameijer is a Dutch author and photographer who has produced spectacular images of orbs; search for his work online.

5ᵗʰ November – Guy Fawkes

Religious strife has been suffered by people for thousands of years and few countries have escaped this in one way or another. Guy Fawkes Night is celebrated on this day each year in the UK with bonfires and fireworks and is linked to when he and a group of accomplices attempted to blow up the Houses of Parliament with gunpowder in 1605. At the heart of this plot lay religious fervour between the Catholic and Protestant faiths.

Today, let us all light a candle and when doing so send a loving thought out to the universe for the people, leaders, rulers and governments throughout the world to be happy and at peace in their own faiths and to encourage tolerance and acceptance of other faiths.

The 19ᵗʰ century Lebanese/American poet Khalil Gibran wrote, "You are my brother. I love you when you bow in your mosque and kneel in your church and pray in your synagogue. You and I are sons of one faith – the spirit."

7th November – Silence and Solitude

In today's society with its merry-go-round life, it's no wonder people face burnout or wish to get off the rollercoaster ride to find a more peaceful balance. However, not everyone is able to relocate their homes and workplaces, reduce their hours of employment or take a sabbatical. We all have so many commitments of one kind or another. Yet there are many other ways of finding balance and peace in our lives and one of them is that of silence and solitude.

Choosing silence as a companion for a few hours can enable our 'monkey brains' to subside, leaving us able to focus better and concentrate on tasks to be undertaken. Occasional peace and stillness in our homes can also add general harmony to its atmosphere and soften its energy. During these times of silence and solitude, thoughts can come and go, as they should, but have a sensible flow to them; we can notice them but choose not to dwell on them. And during these retreat modes our own energies can be nurtured quite naturally, providing a self-healing process.

So today we shall consider ways of achieving periods of silence and solitude, perhaps just twenty minutes each day, in the evening after the children have gone to bed or by rising a little earlier in the morning before the rest of the household. Maybe it would be possible to afford a specifically tailored retreat for a week.

These precious moments act as a balm for our minds and allow our bodies to purr with contentment.

9th November – Feed the Birds

Birds are amazing creatures and a joy to observe, with their different plumages and behaviours. Today, help some of the Earth's creatures and feed the birds, whether at home in your garden, in your local park or at a wildlife reserve.

Depending on where we live, many of our birds are finding it harder to source their food nowadays so extra seeds and water bowls as a regular pit stop for them will be of help; they will then also gradually include this area on their flight path when searching for food.

Birds provide wonderful and inspiring displays for us and their morning chorus and evening farewells are such beautiful sounds; this would be a way of offering our thanks to them. By the way, don't forget to bless the food for them before putting it out.

11th November – Armistice Day

This day marks the end of the Great War in 1918, and ceremonies are held in remembrance of all who have suffered in the many wars of the past. It's an appropriate reminder for us all on this day to spend a little time in quiet and stillness and to meditate for peace throughout the world. A two-minute silence is often observed at 11 a.m.

A book entitled *Few Eggs and No Oranges* contains the diaries of Vere Hodgson during 1940-1945. This is a record of her thoughts and experiences during her time in London during the Second World War when she worked for a philanthropic society; each day she would write about her commute to work, making notes on the areas and buildings that had been bombed, the train delays, the food queues and many other activities of daily life in a home front war zone.

The almost continuous extreme emotions of anger, sadness and fear took their toll of everyone. We should consider these emotions for peoples in countries today throughout the world due to war and terrorist activity, and to counteract these, if only in a small way, we can send out a ripple of compassion and peace instead.

A simple way to do this is to repeat a mantra and link a healing colour with it of light blue, pink or magenta, visualising this as a comforting blanket around the world at night for all to sleep in peace and comfort. The mantra could perhaps be, "Peace in my heart and peace in the world."

Imagining and visualising peace for others is of course difficult if we are not at peace ourselves, so it is important for us to try and feel at peace also in order to expand this to the universe.

13ᵗʰ November – The Feast of Feronia

This day celebrates the Greek goddess Feronia, goddess of wildlife, untamed nature and wilderness; her dedicated shrines were created in the wild places of nature.

Our own wildlife, wilderness and untamed nature, require our protection too so today let's dress up warmly, go out of the town or city and create a little altar in a place of nature. This can be done by making a miniature cairn with stones. Being in stillness, we listen to the country sounds or the sounds of the sea and focus our thoughts on the wild places of the Earth and its wildlife, such as the deserts, mountain ranges, rainforests and the untamed oceans. We visualise them protected and thriving and pray that humanity will look after them.

Whether on a beach or in the countryside, let's take a picnic seeing as it is goddess Feronia's feast day.

Helpful tip: A miniature cairn is a small stack of flat stones piled on top of one another, also known as fairy stacks. Using natural resources in the area for the altar pays respect to the goddess.

15ᵗʰ November – Pine Cone Basket Gift

Start collecting pine cones today and dry them slowly in preparation for a gift at Yule or at Christmas. Two weeks before giving them, place them in an airtight container and sprinkle essential oils of frankincense, cinnamon, orange and clove over them, then tightly close the lid for the cones to be infused with this wonderful blended aroma, evocative of relaxed and cosy winter evenings by a log fire.

When gift packaging the pine cones, they can look exceptional in a small wicker basket wound with a ribbon. As an additional thought, make each of them a special wish-carrying gift for the recipient by tying a small glittery label stating wishes such as peace, love, comfort, security, joy, laughter, wisdom, health, happiness or abundance.

This creates a wonderful personal gift, made with thought, for the people we care about.

Helpful tip: Some people like to decorate their cones too, with glitter or acrylic paints.

17th November – Chrysanthemum, the November Flower

There are many indoor and outdoor varieties of chrysanthemum, first grown in Japan over 2,000 years ago; however, their popularity has blossomed in the 20th century. The Chinese credit chrysanthemums with attracting good luck into the home and a life of ease. If we link this with the chrysanthemum stone, whose pattern looks like a chrysanthemum flower head, there is a double-whammy of luck, abundance and manifesting for opportunities as well as synchronicities.

Today, try a little wishing magic using a chrysanthemum plant, readily available in supermarkets at this time of year. If lucky enough to have a chrysanthemum stone in your crystal collection, use this too.

Place a pot of golden-coloured chrysanthemums on a table, or your home altar, and put the chrysanthemum stone next to it. Light a gold-coloured candle and sit in quiet contemplation, imagining the home over the festive period next month nicely decorated, full of family and friends sharing gifts and enjoying good food. Visualise being able to offer our family and friends good hospitality, given with love and without fear of debt. Also, visualise donating some food to the local food bank to help others at Christmas time. Visualise sending love, gratitude, joy and abundance to all people throughout the world.

Try feeling this vision in heart and soul and in doing so feel how it can make the heart sing and sometimes tears sting our eyes. Say a little thank you prayer to God, to Source or to the energies of the universe, in helping us to achieve this. Let the candle burn down safely and be open to receiving an abundant flow that can be shared.

Helpful tip: Depending on which part of the country you live in, chrysanthemums can be planted out in the spring in sheltered spots and they will continue to thrive in the garden.

19th November – A Wealth Buddha

A wealth Buddha makes a lovely gift. Consider purchasing even just a small wealth Buddha statue, commonly known as the fat or laughing Buddha representing being resplendent with finances and plentiful food, for a special friend. They are found in many stores or garden centres now with a wide variety to choose from. If you get a stone-coloured Buddha it is also possible to paint them in bright abundant colours of crimson and gold, making this a more personal choice of gift.

Don't forget to rub his belly and thank him before giving the gift!

Helpful tip: The Japanese deem the wealth Buddha to be Hotei, the divinity of happiness and wealth, so we should respect this by not placing him on the floor and instead elevate his position to a shelf.

21ˢᵗ November – A Chakra-Coloured Garden

This is a good time to plan our gardens for next year, to grow a range of plants and flowers in chakra colours so that we can be surrounded by the spiritual rainbow spectrum. The American poet Ralph Waldo Emerson wrote, "Earth laughs in flowers" and what a wonderful vision this evokes.

Today, check which colours of plants and flowers are already being grown and plan further ones in readiness for next spring. The following are some examples:

◇ Reds for the base chakra could be poppy, salvia, peony or geranium.

◇ Oranges for the sacral chakra are marigold, Californian poppy and montbretia.

◇ Yellows for the solar plexus chakra are sunflowers, alyssum, primrose and daffodils.

◇ Greens (or pink) for the heart chakra are clarkia, sea pinks and bells of Ireland.

◇ Blues for the throat chakra are cornflowers, forget-me-not, baby blue eyes and the glorious agapanthus.

◇ Indigos for the brow chakra are heliotrope, iris, gentian, grape hyacinth and bluebells. If you intend to add bluebells to your garden, please source the indigenous variety.

◇ Violets for the crown chakra are lavender, catmint and campanula.

Blazes of various chakra colours can be found in petunias, sweet peas, pansy, love-in-a-mist, violas, anemones, carnations, lupins, primulas, hollyhocks, freesias, gladioli, tulips, chrysanthemums, dahlias and clematis.

Helpful tip: Even if you're only able to grow flowers in a small tub then a good idea would be to grow pansies or petunias, small plants in a great variety of colours and so providing the chakra colours within a small area.

23rd November – Channelled Writing

Channelled writings abound throughout history and if we believe that the spiritual, celestial and mystical universe wishes to communicate with us, then perhaps this is one way to enable it. It is not only writing that is channelled, such as in the *Conversations with God* series by Neale Donald Walsch; there are many psychic artists who produce incredible artwork by channelling.

Try this yourself today, alone or with a group of friends, first ensuring that you can't be disturbed, your space is cleansed and you're working with a sense of peace and love. Request the protection and guidance of your guides and angels so that only high vibrational energies can channel – and prepare to be amazed at what comes through.

Just sit quietly with a pencil or pen lightly touching paper, quieten your thoughts and allow your mind to wander to 'the middle distance'. Then clear messages may begin to come into your mind, which you write down; for some people, the pencil even seems almost to move of its own accord.

The last time this was tried in a psychic development group that I attend, two members did receive clear words in their minds, which they wrote down. They are happy for me to pass them on here:

"Hello, I am one that was and is and will be so be it inasmuch as I am able almighty and simply divine which is as it should be something that will come to pass and is brighter and lighter and will not touch what it cannot know that all is well spirit is here and I am going now. Listen well."

The other message was, "I called Ezra. Will help you love."

25ᵗʰ November – Indian Head Massage

This form of massage, also known as champissage, has been practised for thousands of years in India. There one can see three generations of a family conducting champissage upon each other, this being a regular part of their routine life. It has now become a common massage option to choose in beauty parlours and spa hotels in western society, and many therapists add the qualification to practise Indian head massage in their range of skills.

However, it is possible to conduct some Indian head massage techniques on ourselves and it can be performed anywhere. Even when at work and feeling a little stressed, one can carry out a few massage techniques to release the muscles and feel an instant relief. Indian head massage is known to alleviate stress, anxiety, lethargy, tiredness and to relieve headaches. It aids restful sleep, promotes positive wellbeing and concentration, among other benefits.

Today, research Indian head massage and check out the various massage movements that can be carried out on oneself, such as petrissage, effleurage, knuckling, thumb and finger frictions and tapotement, any time the muscles require a little respite.

27ᵗʰ November – Topaz, the Sagittarius Birthstone

Topaz is the crystal for November and is also associated with the astrological sign of Sagittarius. This stone can be blue, golden yellow, pink or clear. If we wish for help in making sense of our life experiences so that we can learn from them and put them into perspective, then topaz is a good crystal to use.

On our life's journey, reflecting upon our experiences from the past and present can bring better awareness of what we have learned to the fore and this is where topaz can help. Research topaz today and consider making a purchase.

Helpful tip: Gemstone quality topaz can be expensive; however, small pieces of blue topaz can be bought much more cheaply.

29th November – Ganesh

Figurines of the elephant-headed Hindu deity Ganesh are often seen in MBS shops for sale and he is considered by many to be the perfect divinity to call on for protection in some aspect of life. Ganesh works for us in this protective way by removing obstacles that can stop us from moving forward.

A popular position for Ganesh is facing the front door entrance, so he is able to stop difficulties from entering the home. Many people can also be seen wearing Ganesh pendants in order to harness his qualities.

However, it is important to remember that balance is required in our lives and, whilst we all like things to flow easily and smoothly, sometimes we do require a little rocky road to help us in making better choices. Another way of looking at this is to think of the sailor who sometimes requires rough seas in order to hone his sailing skills, as continuous smooth waters will not help him to develop.

Today, seek out a Ganesh statue and place him near your entrance.

Helpful tip: If unable to locate a statue today, try placing a picture of Ganesh facing your door in the meantime.

December

The time for holly and mistletoe wreathes, for protection and fertility, for snow, celebrations and feasting. These abound this month for Yule, the winter solstice, for Christmas and the New Year and keep us occupied, so it is important to eat healthily and look after ourselves amongst all these activities. This month we celebrate the light of the returning sun illuminating our path and thus it becomes a focus of renewal in our lives, bringing optimism for future possibilities. Reflections of our achievements in the past year are also released with gratitude and we let go of old emotions in preparation for the new cycle. Mother Earth remains barren and it is still the time of the Crone goddess, so inner reflections on what is important in our lives are relevant in order for us to know what we wish to take forward.

1st December – World AIDS Day

We could spend a little time in special prayer today, lighting a blue candle for healing and thinking about all those suffering from this illness. Wherever they are and whoever they are, send a prayer for them to receive loving help and for the guidance of their families and health workers who assist them. Let's pray that whatever they need for their treatment, physical or psychological, can be provided for them.

Don't forget that Archangel Sandalphon can be entreated to carry our prayer to God. If we're able to, we could join in with any of the specific events taking place nearby for World AIDS Day and express our desire to help. AIDS affects people all over the world, with education and welfare also being necessary in controlling this illness.

3rd December – Turquoise, the December Crystal

The crystal for December is the very popular turquoise, especially favoured by many in the turquoise and silver jewellery that Native Americans create for their tribal designs, to enhance their attractiveness.

The energies of turquoise helps us with inner calm, wisdom, compassion, forgiveness for others and ourself, intuition and meditation. It can also aid us in our spiritual growth. As we continue to progress there may be a time where perhaps our journeys plateau or come to a standstill, and turquoise may be appropriate to use at that time so we can expand again when appropriate.

There will have been many changes occurring for us this year in following and attempting the suggestions in this book, so a turquoise crystal can help us to reinforce our learning on the continuing journey.

5th December – Kathgai Deepam

Around this date is the Festival of Lights, or of Lamps, which is especially celebrated by Tamil Hindus, the timing of which is linked to the moon's phase. The bonding of siblings is an important part of the Festival of Lamps. Indian mythology tells that six celestial nymphs reared six babies who later became one when their mother combined them all together, becoming Lord Muruga.

Kathgai Deepam is therefore a wonderful reminder for us to think of our siblings, or if we don't have siblings then perhaps think of our family unit or our friends with whom we share close bonds. We light a candle, or preferably a lantern, and dedicate it to our siblings, close friends and family and request that the bonds between us all flourish in love and joy. If able to, we could conduct a ceremony of lighting the lantern while with our siblings, family or friends, and make a special occasion of the gathering so that the meaning of the event is experienced by everyone.

7th December – A Money Luck Christmas Decoration

Today, make a decoration to hang on the Christmas tree by taking a gold-coloured drawstring pouch and placing a few silver coins and a haematite crystal inside, ready to hang on the tree. The haematite crystal has magnetising energies and thus helps to draw more silver coins towards us. When hanging the pouch on the tree, express gratitude for the past year followed by thanks for financial abundance in the coming year.

Helpful tip: These decorations make nice, simple token gifts for friends at Christmas – perhaps add in a lottery ticket as well!

9th December – Homeopathy

Homeopathy is a complementary therapy recognised by many and regularly used for oneself and for pets. 'Homeo' in Latin means similar or alike, so homeopathy entails like curing like. It was developed in the late 1700s by a German doctor, Samuel Hahnemann, and rather like essential oils it has become big business, with homeopathic remedies being found in many High Street outlets.

The natural energetic vibrations of the plants and other substances for homeopathic preparations are diluted greatly in pure water; if we consider that the human body is about 70% water then perhaps our energetic make-up melds very well with these preparations, creating a natural habitat for our bodies to begin self-healing with the natural vibrations of the homeopathic remedy. Homeopathy practitioners believe that these remedies work with the body's energy system, helping it to rebalance where necessary.

Our first aid cabinets at home today could contain arnica ointment or tablets for bruising, apis mellifica for insect stings and bites, rhus toxicodendron (commonly known as rhus tox) for alleviating skin rashes and colchicum autumnale for episodes of gout.

Research homeopathy today as it may be an option to consider in the future and one that is natural and gentle for our bodies.

11th December – Anael

With Anael being the angel of love, this is the perfect angel with whom to decorate the Christmas tree or simply to place in our homes this month, perhaps on an angel altar. Anniversaries of traumatic events occur at all times of the year but somehow they always seem to have an added rawness at Christmas, so an angel of love is the perfect choice.

The colour green is associated with Anael, a bright and glorious emerald green, and this would go well as part of the colour for the festive season. Why not be creative today and make an angel figure in the colour green to reflect Anael's love in the world. Let's return to our childhood and use the toilet roll cardboard as the body, cut out bright green card for the wings, use green sequins and green glitter. Let's enjoy ourselves, whether on our own or with children.

When complete, honour this angel's open and unconditional love by placing Anael in a prominent position in the home as a reminder to love greatly.

13th December – Elder Month (25th Nov – 23rd Dec)

In the Celtic calendar, this month is the last of thirteen in the year and of course the winter solstice falls within this time too.

The elder tree is linked with endings and beginnings, life and death, with the white flower as life and the black berries as death. Elder is felt to have healing and protective powers. So, a good all-rounder really. The new Celtic calendar starts on the 24th of December so if there is anything to be released before entering the Celtic New Year, use the elder tree to help with this ending.

Visit the countryside today and find an elder tree to sit near, or with your back resting on its trunk if possible. Petition the elder tree to help in the release of worrying thoughts and concerns, requesting its help in removing any blocks within emotional thoughts, so that forward movement into the new cycle ahead can be made without these weights. Afterwards, honour and thank the elder tree by pouring some blessed water onto its roots, then walk away not looking back.

15th December – The Geminids Meteor Shower

The Geminids meteor shower has a date range of the 6th to the 18th of December. Tonight, dress up warmly and sit outside, watching the night sky to spot the meteors. Each time a meteor is seen, express gratitude for something in your life.

It is so important not to take for granted all that we have in life and all we have achieved, and now that we are nearing the end of the year this is another opportunity to offer our thanks.

Just as at the beginning of this year (see the entry for the 3rd of January), make an event of this meteor display with family and friends and have an al fresco party!

17th December – Joseph of Arimathea

Around this time each year, a sprig of blossom from the Glastonbury thorn, a variety of hawthorn, is cut and sent to the Queen at Sandringham for the breakfast table on Christmas Day.

There are myths suggesting that Jesus, while he was growing up, could have accompanied his uncle Joseph of Arimathea on his trading journeys, perhaps landing near St Michael's Mount in Cornwall to trade in tin and metal goods. Sir Hubert Parry's famous anthem *Jerusalem*, based on a short poem by William Blake, speaks of this:

"And did those feet in ancient time, walk upon England's mountains green…"

It was Joseph of Arimathea who took Jesus from the cross, along with Nicodemus, and legend has it that the Glastonbury thorn grew from Joseph's staff when his party landed on Wirral (Weary All) Hill at Glastonbury, then a sea-bound settlement. The Glastonbury thorn is unique in that it flowers around Easter and Christmas times, depending on weather conditions, so it is significant in the Christian faith.

Consider the richness of myths and legends throughout the world and the wonderful storytelling they evoke for all generations. Storytelling would probably have begun with the ancients in their caves, perhaps relaying their hunting forays to feed the clan using cave paintings as a source of inspiration. Many myths and legends have been relayed by memory, so each generation of storytellers would have omitted parts or expanded on the storylines. There is great learning and wisdom to be gained from these legends, for example Aesop's Fables.

So today, why not write a story to read to members of your family. Base it on your family's experience of a particular day so that a family legend is created. If there are children in the family, you might start with "Once upon a time…" and perhaps end it with "…and the moral of the story is…" Draw illustrations, be creative! Most of all, be ready to recite it to the family on Christmas Day as a verbal gift for them.

Helpful tip: Clarissa Pinkola Estes' book *Women Who Run with the Wolves* is one that may provide some inspiration for your story, in understanding folklore archetypes and their continuing links in today's society.

19ᵗʰ December – Hannukah

This is the Jewish festival of lights to celebrate the rededication of the temple in Jerusalem, when with only a small drop of sacred oil the eternal flame lasted for eight days. The menorah is now part of this celebration in that it holds nine candles, one for each of the eight days and one to light them all. As such it represents the eternal flame.

Today, we could all light a candle, or even nine, to represent the eternal flame of the religion of love and kindness throughout the world, and intend to be mindful of this each day.

21ˢᵗ December – Yule and Saturnalia

Many people celebrate Yule, the winter solstice, with friends at ancient stone sites. This is a good time quietly to contemplate our achievements in the past year and also to acknowledge our gratitude for what we have learned and experienced and of course for the Earth and her continuing nurture. This gratitude is a ripple of love energy being sent out to the universe. It is a time also to request the returning sun to energise and inspire us for the new cycle about to begin.

Another Yule activity for many is that of preparing a Yule log, so today let's revert to a little childhood creativity. Find a round log and colour it with an orange or yellow sun at each end with rays extending to the edges, and embellish it with greenery such as holly and ivy. Write a list of thanks for the past year and a list of wishes for the coming year, and tie these to the log. Sit in peace and quiet for a short while, then place the log onto a fire and watch the smoke carry your thanks and wishes away into the universe.

Moreover, while being creative today, perhaps consider making an orange and clove pomander too as the orange represents the sun and its energy. In aromatherapy, the orange citrus aroma can be uplifting and revitalising to our senses and when combined with the aroma of cloves it produces a warming aromatic effect for our homes.

As tomorrow is Saturnalia, an ancient Roman festival celebrating the winter solstice, perhaps in the spirit of the returning light we could all dress up warmly and have a small fire on the beach or in the garden with friends, roasting chestnuts and with plenty of hot chocolate to keep warm. Your Yule logs could then be burned on this fire.

23rd December – Wassailing

This traditional activity is pagan in origin and very much linked with the apple tree, which pagans deem sacred. 'Wassail' means good health in the Old Saxon language so visiting the apple orchards to chase away bad spirits from the apple trees ensured the good health of the trees and the people. The traditional rite is still carried out in many country communities.

Cider will be poured upon the roots of the oldest tree as an act of honouring it, and in order to scare away any bad spirits one shouts "Huzzah" and makes noises. The wassailers will then visit local houses with their wassail bowl and offer the occupants a drink as a way of joining in with the ceremony. The main traditional ingredient of the wassail bowl was beer, though apple juice can replace beer to keep it alcohol-free and also be in line with honouring the apple tree.

Today, you could enjoy some time with family, friends and neighbours and if there is an apple tree in the garden or nearby then revive the tradition with a wassail ceremony around it, toasting each other with the traditional wassail drink.

The original wassail drink is made with 1 litre of beer (or apple juice), 2 pinches of ground ginger, 2 pinches of ground cinnamon, 2 pinches of ground nutmeg, 100 g of sugar, the juice and rind of a lemon and 3 chopped dessert apples. Place all these in a saucepan and gently simmer, not boil, for approximately ten minutes. Cheers everyone!

25th December – St Stephen

The Christmas carol of Good King Wenceslas centres around a kind king and his page going out into the deep snow and cold of winter to help a poor peasant on the Feast of Stephen. Before being canonised as St Stephen, this man was a deacon in the Jewish faith and one of his tasks was to distribute alms to the poor. However, history tells us that he criticised the hierarchy of his faith in how they administered the teachings of God to the people, and his criticism subsequently led to his trial and condemnation to stoning to death.

St Stephen had faith in a God whom he believed showed mercy, kindness and goodness to all and he expressed his conviction by his actions.

Irrespective of what faith we have, let us all show kindness to others in whichever way we are able. Kindness comes in all manner of wrappings: a kind word to neighbours, donation of food for those struggling, helping with charitable events and so on. We all have kindness within us all, it just has to be let out more often in order to become contagious.

27th December – Ceromancy

Ceromancy is divination by reading the forms that melted wax makes when it enters a bowl of water. Try this today and see what shapes are formed.

Pillar candles are the best to use for this purpose as they collect the melted wax well and it produces a fair-sized shape when it's poured into a bowl of water. When doing this, please be careful as hot wax can possibly drip onto the hands or the table. Ensure the bowl of water is ready nearby, then snuff out the candle and upend it with a steady hand so the collected melted wax pours into the water. It will immediately form into an outline.

It is believed that specific wax shapes have meanings, such as a wheel forecasting travel, and these can be checked out in a book or online. However, try using your own intuition by noting what the shape looks like and how it may resonate with something going on in your life.

Helpful tip: As we are about to enter a new cycle, consider posing a question before pouring the wax, such as, "What should I be mindful of in my life for the coming year?"

29th December – Mirror Work

The entry for the 5th of April suggested adopting a practice of morning affirmations and it described how these may be conducted while standing in front of a full-length mirror. This routine is a very tiny part of what is known as mirror work. Louise L Hay and Dr Robert Holden are great exponents of mirror work and very much believe in the many benefits it can create for us in our lives.

Looking at ourselves in a large mirror helps us to honour ourselves, love ourselves and confirm to ourselves that we deserve this love. So research mirror work today as it may be just what is required in time for the New Year and a new cycle of life.

31st December – New Year Resolutions with Bay Leaves

Instead of the usual New Year resolutions, which often fall at the first hurdle, why not make this action a more meaningful event and ask family and friends to join in? Approaching our New Year's resolutions in a different way will perhaps remain in our memory far better and be a good motivation when our commitment levels begin to lapse.

The smoke from fresh bay leaves when thrown onto a fire is thought to carry our wishes magically out into the universe and thus our resolution has two energies – the energy of our thoughts plus the magical smoke. When throwing the bay leaves into a fire they will crackle and make loud noises like fire crackers, these sounds being caused by the oils within the leaf burning. So for those who like to have firecrackers at a New Year celebration but dislike fireworks, using bay leaves can be an acceptable substitution.

Pick some fresh bay leaves today, preferably at sunrise, and when doing so don't forget to thank the bay tree. In the evening, write your resolution in felt tip on the underside of the leaf (or leaves, if bold enough to make several resolutions) and when everyone is ready throw them all onto the fire at once.

Happy New Year everyone!

Epilogue

"Going on means going far. Going far means returning."

The above is from Lao Tsu's *Tao Te Ching* and it has much resonance with our journey this year if several of the suggestions in this book have been followed.

Going far this year on travels with our internal psyche and touching base once again with our inner child, allowing it to flourish, will have brought about a return to our inner light.

Let us all keep going on and going far.

Bibliography

Bailey, Arthur   Dowsing for Health: the application and methods for holistic healing (W Foulsham & Co)

Byrne, Rhonda   The Secret (Simon & Schuster)

Byrne, Rhonda   The Magic (Simon & Schuster)

Chocron, Dara Sarai   Healing Power of Seashells (Earthdancer Books)

Culpeper, Nicholas   Culpeper's Complete Herbal (Arcturus Publishing)

Dunbar, Jo   The Spirit of the Hedgerow (Local Legend)

Hay, Louise L   You Can Heal Your Life (Hay House)

Hodgson, Vere   Few Eggs and No Oranges (the Diaries of Vere Hodgson 1940-1945) (Persephone Books)

Jirsch, Anne   Instant Intuition (Piatkus)

Julian of Norwich   Revelations of Divine Love (Kegan, Paul, Trench, Trüber & Co) (downloadable at *https://archive.org/details/revelationsofdiv00juliuoft*)

Kaymen, A I   Aura Child (Local Legend)

Matthews, Caitlin   Singing the Soul Back Home: Shamanic wisdom for every day (Connections Book Publishing)

MacKail, Davina   The Dream Whisperer (Hay House)

Ortner, Nick   The Tapping Solution (Hay House)

Parton, Jacquie   Tap Once for Yes (Local Legend)

Peace, Nigel   Spirit Revelations (Local Legend)

Pradervand, Pierre   The Gentle Art of Blessing (Cygnus Books)

Walsch, Neale Donald   Conversations with God (Hodder and Stoughton)

Wilbraham, Janine   Can You Hear Me? (Local Legend)

Williamson, Marianne   A Return to Love (Harper Collins)

See also: New England Journal of Medicine 2003-348.2508-16: Leisure activities and risk of dementia in the elderly.

If you have enjoyed this book...

Local Legend is committed to publishing the very best spiritual writing, both fiction and non-fiction. You might also enjoy:

AURA CHILD
A I Kaymen (ISBN 978-1-907203-71-8)

One of the most astonishing books ever written, telling the true story of a genuine Indigo child. Genevieve grew up in a normal London family but from an early age realised that she had very special spiritual and psychic gifts. She saw the energy fields around living things, read people's thoughts and even found herself slipping through time, able to converse with the spirits of those who had lived in her neighbourhood. This is an uplifting and inspiring book for what it tells us about the nature of our minds.

DAY TRIPS TO HEAVEN
T J Hobbs (ISBN 978-1-907203-99-2)

The author's debut novel is a brilliant description of life in the spiritual worlds and of the guidance available to all of us on Earth as we struggle to be the best we can. Ethan is learning to be a guide but having a hard time of it, with too many questions and too much self-doubt. But he has potential, so is given a special dispensation to bring a few deserving souls for a preview of the afterlife, to help them with crucial decisions they have to make in their lives. The book is full of gentle humour, compassion and spiritual knowledge, and it asks important questions of us all.

A UNIVERSAL GUIDE TO HAPPINESS

Joanne Gregory (ISBN 978-1-910027-06-6)

Joanne is an internationally acclaimed clairaudient medium with a celebrity contact list. Growing up, she ignored her evident psychic abilities, fearful of standing out from others, and even later, despite witnessing miracles daily, her life was difficult. But then she began to learn the difference between the psychic and the spiritual, and her life turned round.

This is her spiritual reference handbook – a guide to living happily and successfully in harmony with the energy that created our universe. It is the knowledge and wisdom distilled from a lifetime's experience of working with spirit.

A SINGLE PETAL

Oliver Eade (ISBN 978-1-907203-42-8)

Winner of the first national Local Legend Spiritual Writing Competition, this page-turner is a novel of murder, politics and passion set in ancient China. Yet its themes of loyalty, commitment and deep personal love are every bit as relevant for us today as they were in past times. The author is an expert on Chinese culture and history, and his debut adult novel deserves to become a classic.

THE QUIRKY MEDIUM

Alison Wynne-Ryder (ISBN 978-1-907203-47-3)

Alison is the co-host of the TV show *Rescue Mediums*, in which she puts herself in real danger to free homes of lost and often malicious spirits. Yet she is a most reluctant medium, afraid of ghosts! This is her amazing and often very funny autobiography, taking us 'back stage' of the television production as well as describing how she came to discover the psychic gifts that have brought her an international following.

Winner of the Silver Medal in the national Wishing Shelf Book Awards.

5P1R1T R3V3L4T10N5

Nigel Peace (ISBN 978-1-907203-14-5)

With descriptions of more than a hundred proven prophetic dreams and many more everyday synchronicities, the author shows us that, without doubt, we can know the future and that everyone can receive genuine spiritual guidance for our lives' challenges. World-renowned biologist Dr Rupert Sheldrake has endorsed this book as "…vivid and fascinating…pioneering research…" and it was national runner-up in The People's Book Prize awards.

These titles are all available as paperbacks and eBooks.
Further details and extracts of these and many
other beautiful books may be seen at

www.local-legend.co.uk

Lightning Source UK Ltd.
Milton Keynes UK
UKOW07f1228071116

287013UK00006B/18/P